The A to Z of
Royal Naval Ships' Badges
1919 — 1989

VOLUME 2
H.M.S. BACCHANTE — H.M.S. BUZZARD

By
B. J. Wilkinson, T. P. Stopford and D. Taylor

Neptune Books

P.O. BOX 61, ORPINGTON, KENT

Dedicated to

Charles John ffoulkes C.B., O.B.E., O.St.John, Hon.D.Lit.Oxon., F.S.A.
Lieut. R.N.V.R. 1914-1918, Hon.Major Royal Marines 1918-1920
First Admiralty Advisor on Heraldry 1918-1936
Born 26th June 1868   Died 22nd April 1947

The Colour Illustrations
These are actual photographs of the sealed patterns for which we are deeply indebted to Devonport Management Ltd., Devonport Royal Dockyard, and also to CS(PS)6b, M.O.D. London, for permission to reproduce them. All of the patterns remain the Copyright of the Ministry of Defence (Navy).

ISBN: 1 870842 02 2

Published by Neptune Books P.O. Box 61 Orpington Kent

Printed by A. G. Bishop & Sons Ltd Cray Valley Road St Mary Cray Orpington Kent

A proportion of the profits from the sale of this volume will be donated to the King George's Fund for Sailors, and we are grateful to Capt. K. Sutherland R.N. for supplying the following outline of the work of the fund.

KING GEORGE'S FUND FOR SAILORS
1 CHESHAM STREET, LONDON SW1X 8NF
Telephone 01-235 2884   Registered Charity No. 226446

Established in 1917 to co-ordinate and control a bewildering number of maritime charities, King George's Fund for Sailors is the central fund for all charities, trusts and funds which care for seafarers and their dependants. Today there are 165 such charities and KGFS exists solely to secure and to give financial support to those whose need is greatest.

Whether they look after the needs of serving or former members of the Royal or Merchant Navies, the Fishing Fleets or the Maritime Support Services, all recognised maritime charities may apply to KGFS for financial help. Most do. Each year, following scrutiny of their applications and accounts, KGFS makes grants totalling almost £1.5 million to more than 100 applicant organisations, thus ensuring that the money is given to those who need it most.

Some need help urgently to meet unforeseen contingencies; others to meet regular and routine commitments. Many do not have the resources to make their own appeals for financial support and depend heavily on KGFS to maintain the level of support they have provided for many years, whether caring for seafarers in homes for the aged or infirm, educating orphans at training ships or schools, or providing for widows left behind after two World Wars, or more recently, the Falklands campaign.

Few seafarers who survived World War II can be below the age of 60 today and many will face retirement and old age in distressing circumstances. To these must be added the problems of today's sailors and fishermen, often exacerbated by sickness, injury and subsequent unemployment. There is already a noticeable increase in demands on KGFS each year and this means an urgent need for a substantial rise in the Fund's income. Increased donations, covenants and legacies are an essential part of existing fund-raising activities to help KGFS face the difficult years ahead.

Donations to the Charity from readers will be very much appreciated, and should be sent directly to the Charity at the above address.

Acknowledgements

We are sincerely grateful and deeply indebted to the following organisations and individuals, whose willing co-operation and enthusiastic assistance, has made the compilation of this volume possible.

Arthur Pote, Clive Birchall, Ray Manley, Dennis Gillings, Charles Sells, Bob Bye, John Wolfenden and John Constantine — Devonport Management Ltd., Devonport Royal Dockyard

Mrs. Sue Netherton — Secretary, Ship's Badges Committee, M.O.D.(N), Bath

David Brown, David Ashby, Alan Francis, and Philip Wilton — Naval Historical Library, M.O.D.(N), London

Sir Walter Verco K.C.V.O., Surrey Herald — Present M.O.D.(N), Advisor on Heraldry

The Librarian and Staff of Colchester Public Library

The Librarian and Staff of Orpington Public Library

Staff of the Reading Room of the Imperial War Museum

Miss Caroline Roberts of the National Maritime Museum

Messrs Vickers Shipbuilding and Engineering Ltd., Barrow-in-Furness for their support.

We would like to express our appreciation for the assistance and superb service rendered by our printers, Messrs A. G. Bishop and Sons Ltd and especially to Chris Bishop and Tom Harrison. Finally, without the support, patience and forbearance of two long suffering wives this book could not have been written. To Anna and Pam, thank you.

We wish to extend our appreciation to the following who have kindly supplied photographs, and in many cases have agreed to waive any copyright fees.

Adrian Vicary	Maritime Photo Library 8 Jetty Street Cromer NR27 9HF	(Acknowledged as MPL)
Ron Forrest	Wright & Logan Ltd 20 Queen Street Portsmouth	(Acknowledged as W&L)
Dr. R. Osborne	World Ship Society 57 Chescombe Road Yatton BS19 4CU	
Mr. McKenzie	Husband's of Bristol 8 St Augustine Parade Bristol BS1 4UU	
Bob Russell	Real Photos Ltd Coombelands House Coombelands Lane Addlestone Weybridge KT15 1HY	
Paul Kemp, Jo Buggins and the Trustees	Imperial War Museum London SW1	
Jim Goss	NAVPIC 64 Gains Road Southsea Portsmouth PO4 QPL	
Rob Gribbin	Skyfotos Ltd Littlestone Road New Romney Kent TN28 8LN	
Len Lovell	FAA Museum Yeovilton	

Messrs. Vosper-Thornycroft Ltd., Mr. L. Van Genderen, Mr. W. Sartori, Dennis Maxted and special thanks to Mrs. Alma Topen of the Glasgow University Archives. We are also very grateful to Mrs. Carol Read for allowing us access to the vast, private photographic collection of her late husband, Lieut.-Cdr. George Read R.N., Mr. Albert Wilkinson, B.E.M., (the writer's father), for permission to use negatives from his collection, and finally Kent Photo News and Clive Woodley for their assistance.

Index

The following patterns have not been included in this volume:—

Bacchus	These will be	Boom Defence	These will be
Bayleaf	described in the	Service Vessels Type	included in the
Black Ranger	volume dealing with	Badge	volume dealing with
Black Rover	Royal Fleet	H.M.Y. Britannia	Miscellaneous
Blue Ranger	Auxiliaries.	Royal Naval Aircraft	badges.
Blue Rover		Yard, Belfast	
Brambleleaf			

Bibliography

Recommended for further reading

English Heraldry	—	Charles Boutell
The Art of Heraldry	—	A. C. Fox-Davies
British Warship Names	—	T. D. Manning & C. F. Walker
Man-o-War Names	—	Prince Louis of Battenberg
British Battles and Medals	—	L. Gordon
Ships of the Royal Navy	—	J. J. Colledge
British Destroyers	—	E. J. March
Heralds of England	—	A. R. Wagner
Civic Heraldry of England and Wales	—	C. W. Scott-Giles
Janes Fighting Ships	—	(Various Editions)
British Warships Since 1945	—	M. Critchley & J. Worth
Shorter Oxford English Dictionary	—	(1933 Edition)
Concise Universal Biography	—	Sir J. A. Hammerton
Fairburn's Crests	—	J. Fairburn
Encyclopaedia Britannica	—	(Twelfth Edition)
Smaller Classical Dictionary	—	Sir William Smith
A Classical Dictionary	—	J. Lempriere

(This work was the original reference for naming of R.N. warships in the 19th century and the original copy used still exists in the Naval Historical Library).

Burke's Peerage	—	(Various editions)
A Biographical Peerage of the Empire of Great Britain	—	J. Johnson
British Battles on Land and Sea	—	Cassell
Nelson's Encyclopaedia	—	Nelson
The Royal Navy Day By Day	—	R. Shrubb & A. Sainsbury
Sea Battles	—	David & Charles

The above list only constitutes a part list of books that we have used to cross-reference and check information researched, but these were consulted more than any others.

General Introduction

This book is the second in a series of twenty volumes which, when completed, will illustrate and describe every badge of the Royal Navy, approved by the Ship's Badges Committee from 1919 to 1989.

Response to Volume 1 has been very encouraging and we have received many letters offering constructive criticisms and suggestions. Numerous readers have requested that we give more information on the derivation of the name and more details of the badge. We have tried to do this in the volume you are about to read, but we are constrained by reasons of space.

(For many of the badges, it would be possible to write a complete book on each one!)

We have also been asked to supply more information on the ships that wore the badges, again we have also tried to do this, but it should be remembered that this is a work on Naval Heraldry and there are very many excellent books available from other publishers, giving far more information on the history of individual ships, than space permits us to give.

We are very privileged to have been permitted to read the minutes of the original Ship's Badges Committee, by the good offices of Sue Netherton, present secretary to the Ship's Badges Committee. Many facts have emerged for the first time and are incorporated in this volume, one of the reasons why the publication has been delayed.

One final point, the reader should constantly bear in mind that details and facts are presented in the light of knowledge, or as they would have appeared, *at the time the pattern was designed.* For example, a badge designed in 1923 makes reference to an industry of a town, and this industry no longer exists, or mentions a dock and the dock has long since closed.

We sincerely hope the reader derives as much pleasure from the reading of this volume, as we have in compiling it.

Barry Wilkinson
Tim Stopford
Derek Taylor

Notes on Text

A standard format has been adopted to make for ease of reference. The name of the ship is at the heading of each entry and the date in brackets behind the name indicates the year of the launch of the first ship of that name (or her naming). The number at the top of the page corresponds with the numbering sequence of the colour illustrations.

The blazon and motto (where recorded) is given under.

The date shown is the date of the approval of the badge by the Ship's Badges Committee; the frame, that of the pattern as originally approved, and the Herald gives the name of the Admiralty Advisor on Heraldry, responsible for the design.

The derivation of the name is given in detail, and is specific to prevent any possible confusion.

The derivation of the badge is given as the Herald intended, with additional information where necessary but, where we have discovered an error, or the derivation of the badge was not given correctly, or omitted completely, we have attempted to the best of our ability to correct the error, or supply the missing information. (For example: Error — H.M.S. Blencathra and H.M.S. Burghead Bay, Omission — H.M.S. Bellerophon and H.M.S. Brilliant.)

The badge heritage lists which ships wore the badge, and shows the type and class of warship, her builder and date of launch, and details of her fate.

Additional information and germane comments will be found in the notes.

Notes on Mottoes

Most mottoes that are in Latin are open to several interpretations. We have followed the Herald's original interpretation, as there is usually an allusion in the motto, either to the name, or the meaning of the name and mis-translation or re-translation into the more modern form, would diminish or eliminate the allusion.

We have used the term 'Not recorded' to indicate that no Official motto for the ship is listed in S.B.C. Records, however, many of the ships concerned did have a motto, but usually composed by the ship's officers and in use only for a single commission. These mottoes are outside the parameters of this work.

Notes on Colours

The language of Heraldry is very constrictive as far as describing the wide varieties of shades of blue, green and red used in the badge designs. Charles ffoulkes used a range of water-colours, produced by Winsor and Newton Ltd., especially adapted for Heraldic use and sold as long ago as 1863. Fortunately this firm is still in existance and details of exact shades are readily available. We include a listing of their range, (with their current numbers in order that the reader can establish for himself the correct shade), later in this book.

It cannot be emphasised strongly enough that the use of every colour in a badge has a definite meaning and was not chosen at random. It also should be remembered that many badges, as produced, differed from the original pattern to some minor or lesser degree in colour, due to the allowance made for a certain amount of 'artistic licence' and certain badges repainted on board ship, due to wear and tear, finished up looking very different from their original appearance.

Notes on Blazons

The criteria for blazons (Heraldic Descriptions), as we understand them are:

1. That the blazon should be couched in such terms and with sufficient detail to enable an artist, with a knowledge of Heraldry, to draw and paint the design, without recourse to an illustration.

2. That the blazons should conform to basic Heraldic rules.

We shall endeavour to do this but, at the same time, keeping the language of Heraldry to a minimum, therefore, we have decided to give the English words for the colours. This has the advantage of attempting to clear the fog of confusion that has previously existed regarding the use of the term 'argent', which can be depicted either silver or white.

To reduce repetition in the text, readers are asked to accept a few established Heraldic usages. For example, unless otherwise indicated in the blazon, all charges face to the dexter (the left as viewed by the observer), the most important area of a shield or badge.

Swords, spears, hammers, axes etc., as well as other objects whose normal aspect is upright, will have their 'business ends' in the chief (the upper area of the badge), the area second in importance of a shield or badge.

Where a sword is blazoned 'proper' it is intended that the colouring be — blade silver, pommel and hilt gold.

We have refrained from explaining the use of barry wavy of white and blue, or blue on its own, when used in a badge design solely to signify the sea or the Royal Navy.

Each Admiralty Advisor on Heraldry have their own particular style, Charles ffoulkes usually gave a definite allusion in the choice of field colour, Sir Arthur Cochrane frequently used blue as a field colour where no allusion to the name other than to the Royal Navy, the sea or the sky was required, Mr. Trappes-Lomax tended to follow suit, whilst the present Advisor on Heraldry, Sir Walter Verco, frequently presents his designs on a plain white field, to provide contrast for the charges placed upon it, unless an allusion is required.

Interpreting the Blazons

A ship's badge is formed from several components. In very much simplified terms one of the designs shown in this volume is examined, piece by piece, to give an example of how the blazons can be fully understood, without a comprehensive knowledge of Heraldry. In the blazons, punctuation is limited to an apostrophe after the field colour and a comma after each colour in the description of the badge.

H.M.S. BACCHANTE

White; Three barrulets wavy in base blue, surmounted by a torch black, enflamed proper, between two sprigs of ivy and four bunches of grapes pendant from chief all proper.

1. The field colour is given first :– 'White'.

2. Next, any charge that is an 'ordinary' which is fully in contact with the field, its number, shape, position and colour:– 'Three barrulets wavy in base blue'.

3. Next, the centrally placed charge:– 'surmounted by a torch black, enflamed proper': this indicates that the black torch with its flames of natural colours, partially overlays the three wavy barrulets.

4. Finally, any other charges placed on the field or upon other charges:– 'between two sprigs of ivy and four bunches of grapes pendant from chief all proper'. This informs the reader that the previously blazoned charge — the torch, is between the sprigs of ivy hanging from the upper section of the badge, each sprig incorporating two bunches of grapes, all depicted in their natural colours of green and purple.

There follows a Glossary containing most of the Heraldic terms used in this book, but we would earnestly recommend that the reader obtains access to some of the many excellent books currently available on Heraldry, in order to obtain a better insight into the colourful and fascinating world of this subject.

A Glossary of Heraldic Terms

Addorsed	—	Back to back.
Affrontee	—	Facing the observer.
Apaumee	—	A hand, glove, or gauntlet, the palm presented towards the observer.
Armed	—	In animals and birds; teeth, claws, tusks, talons and beaks, in arrows; the heads — when shown of a different colour to that of their main component.
Bar	—	A horizontal band approximately one fifth the width of the field.
Barrulet	—	The diminutive of a bar.
Barry wavy	—	Undulating barrulets of alternating colours.
Base	—	The lower part of a field.
Bend	—	A band of approximately one fifth of the width of the field, extending from dexter chief to sinister base, unless specified sinister.
Bendwise	—	Disposed diagonally to the dexter, unless specified sinister.
Beset	—	Surrounded.
Bezant	—	A gold roundel, usually depicted flat.
Billet	—	A small, flat, oblong block, normally depicted vertical.
Caboshed	—	The head of an animal, full face, with no part of the neck showing. (This term is not used for lions, tigers, leopards or foxes.)
Canting Arms	—	Arms which play on the name, giving a pun.
Charge	—	Any object borne upon the field, or upon other charges.
Chief	—	The upper part of the field, usually about one-third.
Chevron	—	An inverted V, with wider spread arms.
Cinquefoil	—	An Heraldic charge of conventional form, having five leaves or petals.
Conjoined	—	Linked or touching.
Couped	—	Cut off cleanly.
Courant	—	Running at full speed.
Cross	—	The cross of St. George.
Cross Patee	—	A cross consisting of a vertical and a horizontal bar, both edges of the four arms increasing in width by a curve outwards from the centre and the extremities of the arms cut square.
Cubit-arm	—	An arm couped below the elbow.
Dexter	—	Pertaining to the right hand, therefore the left side of the shield or badge as viewed.
Displayed	—	Describes the wings of a bird of prey when spread with tips elevated.
Doubled	—	The lining of cloaks and robes.
Ducal coronet	—	A circlet adorned with four strawberry leaves (three visible). This is not the coronet worn by a Duke.
Embattled	—	The battlements of a tower, castle or bridge.
Embowed	—	Curved or bent, or describing an arm flexed at the elbow.
Enfiled	—	Encircled by; a charge passed through a coronet is enfiled by the coronet.
Enflamed	—	Burning, on fire, or engulfed in flames.
Engrailed	—	Edged with small semi-circles with points outwards.
Ensigned	—	Placed immediately above, as though resting upon the upper edge. This term is usually reserved for the positions of crowns or coronets.
Erazed	—	Torn off, so as to present a ragged edge.
Estoile	—	A charge of six wavy rays representing a celestial star, different numbers of rays are stated.
Expanded	—	The wings of birds, other than birds of prey, when spread with tips elevated.

Fess (in)	—	Upon an imaginary horizontal line across the centre of a badge.
Fesswards	—	Pointing to the centre.
Fesswise	—	Disposed horizontally.
Field	—	The surface or background of a badge.
Fimbriated	—	A narrow edging of colour.
Forcene	—	The attitude of a horse when rearing on its hindlegs.
Fructed	—	Bearing fruit, berries, acorns or nuts.
Gorged	—	Encircled about the neck.
Guardant	—	Applied to beasts looking at the observer.
Hurt	—	A blue roundel.
Inclined to Profile	—	The attitude of charges facing at an angle between affrontee and profile.
Increscent	—	A half moon with its horns to the dexter.
Invected	—	Edged with small semi-circles with points inwards.
Inverted	—	Depicted upsidedown.
Issuant (from)	—	Issuing from.
Langued	—	The tongue of a beast or bird.
Martlet	—	The Heraldic Swallow family with tufts of feathers representing legs.
Mascle	—	A voided lozenge.
Middle Base	—	The lower central point of a badge.
Mount	—	An area in base, coloured green, unless otherwise stated. It usually represents a hill.
Mullet	—	A star of five points with straight arms.
Mural crown	—	A coronet in the form of a masoned and embattled wall.
Naiant	—	Swimming.
Nowed	—	Of serpent's tails and cordage when knotted.
Orle (in)	—	A form of inner border not touching the edge of the field.
Palewise	—	Disposed vertically.
Palisado crown	—	A circlet heightened with pointed palisades riveted to the rim, their number varying, normally with seven visible.
Passant	—	Passing, applied to animals walking with dexter forefoot raised.
Pellet	—	A black roundel.
Per fess	—	The division of the field in half, horizontally by colour.
Perspective (in)	—	Charges depicted as if distant.
Pile	—	A narrow triangular shaped charge, normally with point downwards.
Plate	—	A white roundel.
Proper	—	Depicted in its usual or natural colours, but if confusion could arise, the colours used are stated.
Rampant	—	The attitude of an animal erect, having its sinister hind foot on the ground, with the other feet and tail elevated.
Reguardant	—	Looking behind or backwards.
Royal coronet	—	This term has been adopted by the writers to describe the Heraldic open coronet of the younger sons and daughters of the Sovereign, to avoid confusion with the similar Heraldic coronet of the Prince of Wales.
Saltire (in)	—	Crossed diagonally.
Sejant	—	Sitting.
Sinister	—	Pertaining to the left hand, therefore the right side of the shield or badge as viewed.
Slipped	—	The stalk of a plant or flower torn or plucked off.
Statant	—	Standing on all of its legs.
Surmounted (by)	—	Partially covered (by).
Torteau	—	A red roundel.
Traversed	—	Facing to the sinister.
Viroled	—	The banding surrounding bugle horns and trumpets.
Voided	—	With centre removed parallel to outline.
Volant	—	In flight. (Of birds or other winged creatures).

Colour Notes and List

The firm of Winsor and Newton produced a range of watercolours in a boxed set for Heraldic painters as long ago as 1863.

The original colours were as follows:

Azure, Azure (No. 2), Gules, Gules (No. 2), Vert, Vert (No. 2), Purpure, Sable, Or, Or (Substitute), Or (No. 2), Argent, Argent (Substitute), Proper Colour (No. 1), Proper Colour (No. 2), Proper Colour (No. 3), plus Indian and Black Ink. (Azure = Blue, Gules = Red, Vert = Green, Purpure = Purple, Sable = Black, Or = Gold and Argent = Silver.)

Production followed, to an H.M.S.O. order, of a range of colour blocks and this range would have been made available to Charles ffoulkes. The full listing of these (and their present-day number from the Winsor & Newton range of Artists' Water Colours) are listed below.

H.M.S.O. Number	Name of Colour	Winsor & Newton Number	H.M.S.O. Number	Name of Colour	Winsor & Newton Number
33-11	Brown Madder	007	33-33	Medium Chrome Yellow	015
33-12	Burnt Roman Ochre	No longer available	33-34	Neutral Tint	032
33-13	Burnt Sienna	008	33-35	Paynes Grey	034
33-14	Burnt Umber	009	33-36	Pink	089
33-15	Cadmium Deep Orange	081	33-37	Prussian Blue	036
33-16	Carmine (unbleachable)	094	33-38	Prussian Green	037
			33-39	Purple	038
33-17	Chinese White	011	33-40	Not allocated	
33-18	Cobalt Blue	066	33-41	Queens Green	055
33-19	Crimson Lake	017	33-42	Raw Sienna	040
33-20	Carmine (bleachable)	001	33-43	Raw Umber	041
33-21	Cyanine	018	33-44	Scarlet Lake	044
33-22	Egyptian Blue	019	33-45	Sepia	045
33-23	Emerald Green	054	33-46	Steel	047
33-24	French Blue	068	33-47	Stone	No longer available
33-25	Gamboge	069			
33-26	Hookers Green	070	33-48	Ultramarine	096
33-27	Indian Red	318	33-49	Vandyke Brown	050
33-28	Indian Yellow	024	33-50	Not allocated	
33-29	Indigo	025	33-51	Venetian Red	051
33-30	Not allocated		33-52	Veridian	077
33-31	Iron Oxide	No longer available	33-53	Vermilion	097
			33-54	Veronese Green	No longer available
33-32	Light Red	082	33-55	Yellow Ochre	059

In a future volume we will include a full-colour chart of the above range of paints.

We are very grateful to Mr. T. W. Bokenham, S4C, Her Majesty's Stationery Office, Norwich, and Mr. Richard Goodban of Messrs Winsor & Newton Ltd., Wealdstone, for their invaluable assistance in compiling the above list.

We are also compiling a listing of translation of the above colours into oil-based paints, (with which the actual badges were painted), and this will be published in a full-colour chart with B.S.C. Numbers in a future volume.

Research is being undertaken to establish the colour range in use by the Herald painters of Sealed Patterns at the College of Arms from 1936 to the present day and this information will be given in due course.

History of Royal Naval Badges (Part Two)

'When not historical of the past, it is the office of all true Heraldry to be historical for the future.'

Charles Boutell M.A. 1863

Since the publication of volume 1, the original minutes of the Ship's Badges Committee have been made available to the writers through the kindness of Mrs. Sue Netherton, Secretary to the present Ship's Badges and Names Committee. These records are so important and the information contained in them is not generally known, therefore we are transcribing complete extracts from them, with our comments and additional information in italics in brackets.

Once the decision had been made to establish a standing committee to regularise ship's badges and to ascertain their format, the next stage was to establish a method and the location of manufacture. On the 2nd of January 1919 it was decided that priority for the supply of badges would be given to ships under construction and that the year of launch of the first ship to bear the name would be added to her badge. *(This was not proceeded with, as will be seen, but explains why a date appears on several early badge designs.)* As mentioned in Volume 1, A.W.O. No. 178 of 1919 requested that Commanding Officers of ships with existing badges should give a description of them to the S.B.C. in order that their suitability for continued use could be ascertained. The Committee, in order to approve these designs were guided by the following general principles:–

1. To avoid the use of portraits.

2. To use a cognisance of a person, country or town wherever possible.

3. For mythological names, to use heads distinguished by attributes.

At a conference held by the S.B.C. on the 14th of January 1919, detailed discussions were held regarding the manufacture and size of the various shapes of badges. Charles ffoulkes explained the stages of the badge as then manufactured, i.e. a design first prepared by himself, which would then be modelled in Plasticine. From this Plasticine model a plaster cast would be taken and sent to the Brass Foundry or Dockyard, who would then produce a cast badge, retaining the original plaster model. It was decided that two modellers would be obtained by Mr. ffoulkes who would prepare the model on receipt of the design from him. These modellers would also prepare the plaster cast and send it to Mr. ffoulkes, who would arrange for it to be despatched by the Admiralty to the Brass Foundry or Dockyard selected to undertake the work. It was also agreed that these modellers be permitted to make additional plaster casts of the badges that they could sell to Officers and other interested parties, this being considered a 'prerequisite' that would tend towards reducing the cost to the Admiralty, of production. The question of employing these two modellers was then considered, and it was agreed that the best course to adopt was that they should be paid an agreed sum per badge, in addition they would be entitled to such sums as might be realised by the private sale of plaster casts of the same, this being the preferable course to appointing them as Civil Servants on fixed salaries. The Committee next proceeded to consider by whom the brass castings should be made. It was stipulated that a high level of workmanship was required and also that the Firm selected should be in London, so as to be in the closest possible touch with the Committee. It was also suggested that the work should be carried out in one of H.M. Dockyards, Chatham being preferred for the reason stated above. Following this conference a further proposal was made by Mr. ffoulkes on the 18th of January as follows:–

As an alternative to the foregoing proposals, the whole of the work connected with the supply of badges might best be carried out by an H.M. Dockyard (Chatham is preferred), the designs being supplied by Mr. ffoulkes and sent to the Dockyard through the usual official channels. In that event, it is thought that the badge would be carved in wood in the first place, instead of being modelled in plasticine, from which the brass casts and plaster casts would be taken. Assuming that the work is undertaken in its entirety by Chatham Dockyard, as suggested, it is desirable that the wood craftsmen employed in carving the wooden pattern should be capable of carving human figures, animals, birds, etc., and that the technique and workmanship throughout, i.e. carving, casting and colouring, should be of the highest standard.

On the 29th of January 1919 the Committee approved that the private supply of castings of ship's badges should be made only through the C.O.s of the ships concerned, pending a decision for the central manufacture of all the badges. Two other interesting points were discussed during this meeting, firstly a suggestion by Cdr. B. Freeman of H.M.S. Woolwich that ship's badges should be worn on the uniform. The Committee replied that this proposal was beyond their scope. The second proposal they considered was from the Chester Herald, who suggested that the Admiralty should consult the College of Arms with regard to the design of ship's badges. The Committee thought this was undesirable, if not impossible, owing to the extent of the work and the need for constant intercommunication. *(Charles ffoulkes made no charge for his work on designing badges, the money available to the Committee for badges was very limited and therefore, at that time, the cost of using the services of the College of Arms would have been prohibitive.)*

(The Committee at this time consisted of the Director of Naval Equipment, Commander Holden R.N. (D.N.E. Dept.), Charles ffoulkes and Mr. Laughton, the Admiralty Librarian.)

The sizes of the various badges were decided upon at this time and were laid down as follows:–

Battleships and Battlecruisers *(Capital Ships)*
Ship's Badge: 26½″ overall height, 22¾″ overall width.
Weight: 80 lbs. *(Cost: £13.0.0.)*
Boat Badge (Large): 7″ dia. Weight: 8 lbs. *(Cost: £2.10.0.)*
Boat Badge (Small): 5½″ dia. Weight: 5 lbs. *(Cost: £2.2.0)*

Cruisers
Ship's Badge: 20⅞″ overall height, 16¾″ overall width.
Weight: 36 lbs. *(Cost: £8.0.0.)*
Boat Badge (Large): 7⅝″ high, 7⅝″ wide.
Weight: 8 lbs *(Cost: £2.10.0.)*
Boat Badge (Small): 5½″ high, 5¾″ wide.
Weight: 5 lbs. *(Cost: £2.2.0.)*

Auxiliaries
Ship's Badge: 17⅞″ overall height, 19⅛″ overall width.
Weight: 36 lbs. *(Cost: £8.0.0.)*

Boat Badge (Large): 8″ high, 8″ wide.
Weight: 8 lbs. *(Cost: £2.10.0.)*
Boat Badge (Small): 6½″ high, 6½″ wide.
Weight: 5 lbs. *(Cost: £2.2.0.)*

Destroyers
Ships Badge: 15⅜″ overall height, 10″ overall width.
Weight: 33 lbs. *(Cost: £7.5.0.)*
Boat Badge (Large): Not designed.
Boat Badge (Small): 5½″ high, 5″ wide.
Weight: 5 lbs. *(Cost: £2.2.0.)*

(The cost of the badges are given in pounds, shillings and pence.)

(The main difference between ship's badges and boat's badges, apart from their size, was that only the ship's badge would be made with name panel inserted in the frame at the top of the badge and a Naval crown placed upon it.)

(The next Committee meeting took place on the 26th of March 1919.)

At this meeting it was agreed that Cdr. Drummond should be appointed to succeed Cdr. Holden. Correspondence with the College of Arms was discussed, especially their invitation for a representative of the Admiralty to call on the Garter King-at-Arms. The Naval Secretary informed the Committee that he would call and show him the designs of Charles ffoulkes. It was thought that for the future it would be enough that the College of Arms be sent a photograph of each badge with a blazon. A tender was received from Messrs. Swan Hunter for the manufacture of badges and after some discussion the Committee agreed that a flat rate was necessary. *(As mentioned in the first part of this history, it was always envisaged by Charles ffoulkes that Swan Hunter would make badges for the R.N.)* The subject of tompions was discussed and it was decided that these would remain unofficial, (i.e. not paid for by the Admiralty), but that if ships wish to provide themselves with them, they should follow the design of the badge approved by the Admiralty. It was decided that the date of the first ship to bear a name would not be included in the badge and finally it was decided in future that the design of a badge for a new ship should be submitted with the project.

(The next meeting of the Committee was held on the 30th of April 1919).

It was agreed that ships be allowed to make their own badges, provided that they work from designs approved by the Committee and the Controller and that tracings of approved designs be sent to the ships applying. *(Manufacture of official badges had still not commenced at this date.)* It was also agreed that ships applying for official badges be given them immediately after ships building and that no provisional designs were to be sent out. *(The Commanding Officer of a ship with an existing unofficial badge could, if he so wished, retain it for the duration of the ship's commission, provided that it conformed to the guidelines of the Committee. An Officer appointed to commission a ship with an existing unofficial badge could also retain it and this explains why H.M.S. Vanoc, an Admiralty 'V' Class Destroyer served from 1919 until 1945 without ever being granted an official badge, the only ship of her class to do this. Several other ships, mainly Minesweepers, also long-serving, did not have an official badge for the same reason.)*

During this meeting it was decided that no symbolic badge design being possible for a ship, the crest of the first officer to command may be used. Some Australian Destroyers having applied for badges, it was decided that they should be treated as ships of the R.N., i.e. that they should receive their badges as a free gift.

(H.M.A.S. Stalwart, H.M.A.S. Anzac, H.M.A.S. Tattoo, H.M.A.S. Success, H.M.A.S. Swordsman and H.M.A.S. Tasmania.) It was estimated that the total cost of casting and painting all of the badges required would be from £13,000 to £14,000, this estimate being formed before the last stop of new construction. *(In 1919, a large number of ships under construction or on order were cancelled, mostly Destroyers.)* Messrs. Swan Hunter estimated that it would take from 2 to 3 years to cast all the badges required, without sub-contracting and it was suggested that it might be better to divide the contract, giving capital ships to one firm, cruisers to another and so on. It was then agreed that other firms be invited to tender for the contract.

(The next meeting of the Committee took place on the 29th of July 1919.)

The minutes of the 30th of April were read and approved. Charles ffoulkes mentioned that the carvings for badges were being made by Messrs. Martyn of Cheltenham, *(Royal Warrant Decorators to H.M. King George V)*, the contract for casting having been placed with Messrs. Swan Hunter. He stated that it was now under consideration of the Controller's Dept., whether Swan Hunter's should proceed with the contract, the first sample of their work having been unsatisfactory. *(The writers have inspected many badges made by this firm and they are all well-executed. No information is known regarding the fault of this first badge.)* Discussions were held regarding the Captain's Ship's Book. It was agreed that a copy of the badge design would be inserted with Battle Honours granted, with a copy to be held by the Committee for future amendment.

Designs for several badges were approved. *(It is appropriate to mention here that a full Committee was not originally called upon to pass new badge designs and by the date of this meeting approximately 20 of Charles ffoulkes' designs had been approved.)*

The proposed design for a badge for H.M.S. Warspite was discussed but not resolved. *(This badge design was the subject of much discussion and the full story will be given in the badge entry for this ship in the appropriate volume.)*

(The next meeting was held on the 9th of October 1919.)

It was agreed that on grounds of economy the name panel and crown would definitely be omitted from Boat Badges but not the Ship's Badge. *(The dimensions and weights, costs etc. of the badges given earlier comply with this decision.)* It was also agreed that a revision of the existing estimate of cost be undertaken due to the reduction in the size of the Fleet. *(Many badge designs were approved, destined never to be carved, as large numbers of ships were taken out of service and scrapped or laid up during this period.)* Objections were also raised regarding the provision of the frames around the badges but it was felt that it was important to retain them in order to provide protection to the design.

The next meeting of the full Committee took place on the 6th of January 1921. *(No full meeting of the S.B.C. took place in 1920 but numerous badge designs were approved during the year.)*

It was agreed that Cdr. Coleridge should succeed Cdr. Drummond.

It was pointed out that the sum of £7,000 voted under the 1920-1 Estimates for the making of badges had not been spent and that a considerable part of it would have to be surrendered on the 31st of March. It was therefore agreed under the circumstances that Messrs. Martyn should be asked to push on with the work as much as possible.

It was agreed that for the time being, save in exceptional cases, badges for small craft be postponed, the line being drawn below T.B.D.s *(Destroyers)* and large auxiliaries.

Since the last meeting the procedure for the provision of badges has been approved and this has been issued to the Fleet by A.F.O.3541/20. *(This AFO is not reproduced as it only outlines in detail the procedure for ships to make application directly to Chatham to obtain badges and will be published in full, with all of the others applicable to badges, in an Appendix later in this work.)*

(Many decisions were made between the dates of the full Committee meetings, one of the most important was a decision to direct that all ship's badges were to be cast and painted henceforth in H.M. Dockyard, Chatham; the official date of the commencement of the manufacture of badges in that Dockyard was the 1st June 1921.)

(The next meeting took place on the 4th of August 1921.) The minutes of the last meeting were read and approved.

A report was made showing that the designing of badges and the finding of mottoes for ships of the Post-War Fleet was almost complete, 243 out of a total of about 250 having been approved, the small remainder being in hand. Also, that of these designs, 158 had been sent to the carvers, *(Messrs. Martyn),* before the 22nd of June 1921; and that on that same date 81 sets of carvings had been sent by Messrs. Martyn to Chatham. By the end of July they had completed the carvings from all of the drawings they had received, but these later sets had not been forwarded to Chatham as the work of casting was proceeding slowly there and the yard apparently could not with advantage, undertake more work. To the end of July, Chatham had completed for issue only two sets of castings of badges. *(H.M.S. Tiger and H.M.S. Wishart.)*

It was agreed that the Controllers attention should be drawn to the slowness of output of badges from Chatham and asked to suggest means whereby this could be hastened. *(Chatham Dockyard, in common with all other yards in the country, had been forced to lay off a large proportion of their work-force at this time. From June 1918 until June 1923, only one ship was launched at Chatham, the submarine X-1.)*

The question of the desirability of renaming H.M.S. Whitley was mentioned, but in view of the decision reached on C.Sec.S.15637/19, it was agreed not to raise the question again, but since the date of that paper, Mr. Whitley having been elected Speaker of the House of Commons, to give the ship the Speaker's Mace as a badge. It was felt that if ever the ship-name 'Speaker' should be revived in the Navy, this badge would belong by right to the ship bearing it; but that this was not likely to happen during the lifetime of H.M.S. Whitley, whose name would not be repeated. *(H.M.S. Whitley, an Admiralty 'W' Class destroyer, should have been named H.M.S. Whitby, after the town in East Yorkshire, but was launched by Doxford in 1918 with the wrong name. This at first caused a problem in finding a suitable derivation for the name, but a prominent M.P. at the time, the Rt. Hon. Mr. John Henry Whitley, was deputy Speaker and Chairman of Committees from 1911 until 1921, when he was appointed Speaker of the House of Commons. He was best known as the originator of the Whitley Councils, set up as conciliation boards in industry and the name of the ship was left unchanged in his honour. The design for the badge was submitted for approval on the 13th of June 1921 and approved on the 29th of July 1921. This badge is also notable for the fact that although the Committee had directed that no two ships of different names would wear the same badge, but in this instance provision was made by them for this to occur and when the Escort Carrier H.M.S. Speaker was commissioned in 1943 she wore this badge.)*

(The next meeting took place on the 13th of October 1921.)

In order to save time the minutes of the last meeting were not read but Mr. ffoulkes informed the Committee that the output of badges from Chatham is now satisfactory. *(Additional labour had been allocated by the yard.)*

(Questions of copyright and a proposed exhibition of badges to be held at the premises of Gieves in London were discussed also a request from Gale and Polden Ltd. to reproduce badge designs in letterheads etc.)

A letter, GD319/21, was read concerning the badge for H.M.S. Iron Duke and referred for written remarks. *(This badge showed the Crest of the Duke of Wellington and objections were raised because the 1st Bn. of The Duke of Wellington's Regiment (West Riding) had made prior claim to this crest and derived their cap-badge from it.)*

(The next meeting took place on the 1st November 1921.)

The minutes of the meetings of the 4th August and the 13th of October were approved.

Arrangements were made regarding the forthcoming exhibition of badges at Gieves and an entrance charge of one shilling plus tax was agreed. *(This exhibition took place at Gieves Gallery at 22 Old Bond St., London in December 1921. Fifteen completed castings and ninety-eight carvings were displayed and Gieves published a catalogue of the designs with blazons and other details.)*

Regarding the badge for H.M.S. Iron Duke it was agreed to use a design featuring the head of the Duke of Wellington in profile, to be cast if possible from the unofficial badge already in use. *(This was done and provided an example of an official badge identical with the unofficial one.)*

The Chairman raised the question as to how long the Committee should continue to exist. It was noticed that the Board's instructions to the Committee included the dealing with War Honours, which the Committee had hitherto postponed until all the badges required could be issued. *(We stated earlier that the subject of War Honours or Battle Honours, although an integral part of the work of the Committee, would not be dealt with in this work as this subject is worthy of a book on its own.)*

At this time a further problem was resolved with regard to the manufacture of Boat's Badges. Many of the designs showed a charge facing to the left or to the right and a pair of badges cast from the same pattern would result in one of the badges facing the wrong way when affixed to the boat. It was decided therefore that two carvings would be made for the boat-badges that were 'handed', in order that they could be cast as pairs, so that when a pair of them were in place, one on either side of the boat, they would both face in the same direction.

Charles ffoulkes kept an index system for his badge designs, giving each of them a number, commencing with AAH 001 (H.M.S. Warwick), and writing this number in the top right hand corner of the patterns. This number has unfortunately been cut off many of the patterns whilst in the care of H.M. Dockyard, Chatham in order that they would fit into a standard filing system, (on some of them, even the motto has been removed) but many of these numbers are known. In the next volume we shall include a listing of the numbers ascertained to date, with the names of the ships and this will provide a listing of all of the designs passed by the Committee, during the tenure of Charles ffoulkes as Admiralty Advisor on Heraldry.

In volume three we will take the History of Badges up to the time of the appointment of Sir Arthur Cochrane, Clarenceaux King-of-Arms, as the Official Advisor on Heraldry to the Admiralty in 1936.

SWAN HUNTER

RIGHT FIRST TIME – RIGHT ON TIME

Our Business is Maritime Defence, from Concept to Completion,
Integrating Design, Manufacture and Through-Life Support
for the Defence Industries and Navies of the World.

THE
BADGE
DESCRIPTIONS

Blazon: White; Three barrulets wavy in base blue, surmounted by a torch black, enflamed proper, between two sprigs of ivy and four bunches of grapes pendant from chief also proper.

Motto: Not recorded.

Date: 20.2.1968   **Frame:** Standard

A.A.H.: Capt. E. M. C. Barraclough RN

Derivation of Name:
This was originally a 'prize-name', as the French *'Bacchante'* was captured by H.M.S. Endymion on the 25th of June 1803 and served in the Royal Navy as H.M.S. Bacchante until 1809. The name originates from Roman Mythology: a Bacchante (translated literally as 'frenzied woman'), was a priestess or female votary of Bacchus, the Roman god of the vine.

Derivation of Badge:
The wavy blue and white of the lower field represents the sea, indicating a naval design, whilst the upper part of the field is white, to provide contrast for the charges placed upon it. Classical sculptors quite frequently depicted Bacchantes carrying a thyrsus (an ivy-entwined staff), bearing torches or carrying bunches of grapes in their hands.

Badge Heritage:
1. A 'Leander' Class Frigate, built by Vickers-Armstrong Ltd., launched in 1968 and transferred to the Royal New Zealand Navy as *H.M.N.Z.S. Wellington* in 1982.

Notes:
This is a curious choice of badge design, as it holds no martial significance, merely alluding to the legendary orgies of drunken revellers! On a serious note, a previous ship of the name served with distinction at Cattaro in 1814, whilst another was present at Heligoland in 1914, either of which could have inspired a better design.

Navpic   8th June 1972

Blazon: Red; A sun radiant gold, rising from clouds white, charged with a horseshoe inverted black.

Motto: Not recorded

Date: 5.7.1941   **Frame:** Standard

Herald: Sir A. Cochrane.

Derivation of Name:
One of Yorkshire's oldest foxhound hunts is known as 'The Badsworth' and it takes its name from the village of Badsworth, which lies south of Pontefract. The hunt, as now constituted, has been in existence since 1720 and holds regular meets at Barnsley, Doncaster, and Wakefield, as well as Badsworth. The name was chosen in 1940 for one of the eighty-six 'Hunt' Class Escort Vessels.

Derivation of Badge:
The huntsmen wear a uniform consisting of a red coat faced with a blue collar. The red field of the badge denotes the main colour of this uniform, whilst the golden sun, rising from white clouds, is from the Arms of the Bright family of Badsworth, denoting that it was a Mr Thomas Bright who founded the pack and held the Mastership until 1735. The black horseshoe is a direct reference to the sport of hunting from horseback.

Badge Heritage:
1. A 'Hunt' Class Type II Escort Vessel (later Destroyer) built by Cammell Laird, launched in 1941 and transferred to the Royal Norwegian Navy in 1944.

Notes:
As the first vessels of this class to be ordered were not at first classed as Destroyers, their badges were in a diamond-shaped frame, denoting their original classification as Auxiliary Vessels for the purpose of the badge design.

MOD(N)   circa 1942

Blazon: White; Two bugle-horns with mouths inclined to middle base supported by their strings all blue, held in the hand of a dexter cubit arm erect proper.

Motto: Not recorded.

Date: 14.12.1953   **Frame:** Standard

Herald: Sir A. Cochrane

Derivation of Name:
Bamborough, (or Bamburgh), Castle stands in the village of Bamburgh, Northumberland, not far from Berwick-upon-Tweed. It is reputed to have been built by Ida, the first King of Northumbria, in 547 A.D. and was originally called Bebbanburgh, after his wife, Bebbe. The castle has massive strength and dignity, rising high out of a mass of rock to 150 feet above sea level.

Derivation of Badge:
The design of this badge makes reference to part of the long history of this castle. Queen Elizabeth I appointed Sir John Forster to be its Governor and to hold the office of Warden of the Eastern Marches*.

The castle remained in this family until 1715, when Tom Forster, Sir John's descendant, forfeited all rights and lands as punishment for his participation in the Jacobean Uprising, which occurred in that year. The two blue bugle-horns are said to be derived from the Arms of Sir John Forster, whilst it is thought that the arm denotes the 'arm of the Law', to indicate Sir John's office of Warden.

Badge Heritage:
1. A 'Castle' Class Corvette (later Frigate), built by J. Lewis, launched in 1944 and sold for scrapping in 1959.

Notes:
*The Marches referred to were potentially hostile borders between England and Scotland and also between England and Wales. Wardens were appointed by the reigning sovereign to keep order and prevent border skirmishes.

The long interval between the building of this warship and the grant of her badge is explained by the fact that a decision was made by the Ship's Badges Committee on the 7th of July 1942 that Corvettes would not be granted badges due to the sheer numbers involved. It was stated at the time that this decision would be reviewed post-war. Consequently, this warship was reclassified as a Frigate, along with her surviving sister-ships and they were granted badges.

Blazon: Barry wavy of four white and blue;
A griffin sejant red, armed and langued blue, supporting with its dexter talon a civic mace gold.

Motto: Not recorded

Date: 21.8.1940   **Frame:** Diamond

Herald: Sir A. Cochrane.

Derivation of Name:
Bangor is a City in Carnarvonshire, North Wales, situated near the northern entrance to the Menai Strait. Its history dates back to the 6th Century, when a Celtic monastery was founded there. It should be emphasised that the name honours this city, not the Bangor in County Down, Northern Ireland, even though the ship was built in Northern Ireland.

Derivation of Badge:
The badge shows a red griffin holding a mace all on a field of barry wavy. The barry wavy indicates the sea in reference both to the usage of the badge and also to the location of the town honoured by the name. The red griffin is taken from the Crest of the Arms used by the Corporation of the city, whilst the gold mace is from the shield of the same Arms. The City of Bangor did not have a grant of Arms and used part of the Arms of the See of Bangor, modified by placing a civic mace diagonally upon the original Arms.

Badge Heritage:
1. A 'Bangor' Class Fleet Minesweeper, built by Harland & Wolff, launched in 1940 and transferred to the Royal Norwegian Navy in 1946.

Notes:
This warship gave her name to a class of Minesweepers and those that served in the Royal Navy were all after named coastal towns in the United Kingdom.

Blazon: Blue; A goat statant white, within two branches of laurel bowed and conjoined in base gold.

Motto: Not recorded.

Date: 11.8.1944   **Frame:** Standard

Herald: Sir A. Cochrane

Derivation of Name:

This name commemorates the Battle of Barfleur, which was fought off Cap Barfleur on the 19th May 1692 by a combined British and Dutch fleet, against a French fleet under the command of the Comte de Tourville.

   This battle and the battle of La Hogue that followed, finally dashed the hopes of the exiled James II of winning back the throne of England under the patronage of King Louis XIV of France. The name was selected in 1943 for one of a class of Fleet Destroyers that were all named after notable sea and land battles involving British forces.

Derivation of Badge:

The badge shows a white goat between two branches of laurel all on a blue field. The combined allied fleet was under the command of Sir Edward Russell, Admiral of the Red, flying his flag in H.M.S. Britannia. For his conduct of the Battle of Barfleur, (and La Hogue), he was raised to the peerage on the 7th May 1697 and created Baron Shingay, Viscount Barfleur and Earl of Orford. The white goat is from his Arms and the two golden branches of laurel are used to denote a victory at sea.

Badge Heritage:

1. A 'Battle' Class (First Group) Fleet Destroyer, built by Swan Hunter Ltd, launched in 1943 and sold for scrapping in 1966.

Notes:

H.M.S. Barfleur was the first of the class to be completed (in 1944) and saw brief active service with the British Pacific Fleet.

   On a point of interest, William the Conqueror sailed to invade England in 1066 from the port of Barfleur.

Skyfotos   circa 1954

Blazon: Blue; A wyvern erect gold, gorged with a ducal coronet silver, in its mouth a sprig of laurel proper.

Motto: Tout Bien Ou Rien. (All Good Or Nothing.)

Date: 25.10.1919   **Frame:** Circular

Herald: C. ffoulkes

Derivation of Name:
This name commemorates Admiral Sir Charles Middleton, (1726-1813), Controller of the Navy from 1778 until 1790. He was appointed First Lord of the Admiralty by Lord Pitt in 1805 and although he remained in that office for only one year, some of the credit for the swift measures taken against the French before the Battle of Trafalgar belongs to him. He was raised to the peerage as Lord Barham the same year.

Derivation of Badge:
The field colour, blue, is one of the colours of the Arms of Lord Barham, whilst the gold wyvern is one of his supporters. As displayed in his Arms, this beast has a thistle in its mouth and is not collared. The design of the badge has substituted a sprig of laurel for the thistle. This charge is used in Naval Heraldry to denote a sea victory — in this instance the Battle of Trafalgar and denotes Lord Barham's part in it. The ducal coronet has been added to the neck of the beast to record his peerage.

Badge Heritage:
1. A 'Queen Elizabeth' Class Battleship, built by J. Brown Ltd, launched in 1914 and lost on the 25th of December 1941, when she was torpedoed by U-331. She was struck by four torpedoes and blew up after capsizing. 56 officers, including her Captain, Capt. G. C. Cooke R.N., 658 ratings and 134 marines were lost.

Notes:
The motto of the ship is also that of Lord Barham.

The Official Badge approved for the ship was not worn and throughout her life she wore as her badge the complete shield from the Arms of Lord Barham, namely per fess gold and blue, a lion rampant, armed and langued red, within a double tressure all counterchanged. This design was worn on her bridge screen, although the official design was used for her boat's badges. The unofficial badge that was worn dates from the third ship of the name, (a 3rd Class Cruiser that served from 1891 until 1914). It is difficult to see why the adoption of this badge by the Battleship was permitted, particularly when, as in this case, the ship was consulted prior to the submission and approval of an official design.

There were numerous other examples of disregarding the official badge, as will be seen throughout this work.

Glasgow University Archives — Scottish Record Office

circa 1916

Blazon: Red; The head of a dapple-grey horse erazed reguardant proper, collared black, thereon a rose gold, barbed proper, between two escallops gold, all within two fronds of palm bowed and conjoined in base also gold.

Motto: Not recorded.

Date: 21.2.1946   **Frame:** Standard

Herald: Sir A. Cochrane

Derivation of Name:
This name commemorates the Battle of Barrosa, which was fought on the 5th of March 1811, during the Peninsular War. A British force, in brigade strength, under the command of Lt.-Gen. Sir Thomas Graham, (1748-1843), defeated a much larger force of French troops that were under the command of Marshal Victor. Although this battle was in reality only a small skirmish, it was significant in that it was the first defeat inflicted upon French land forces during the campaign. Sir Thomas Graham was raised to the peerage in 1813 and created Lord Lynedoch.

Derivation of Badge:
The red field of this badge is used to denote the British Army, as red is its traditional colour. The horse's head is derived from the dexter supporter to the Arms of Lord Lynedoch, which is a horse. A black collar has been added to the design, with two gold escallops and a gold rose placed upon it. This collar is derived from the Arms of Lord Lynedoch, which show in chief black, a rose gold, between two escallops gold.

Badge Heritage:
1. A 'Battle' Class (2nd Group) Fleet Destroyer, built by J. Brown Ltd, launched in 1945 and sold for scrapping in 1978.

Notes:
H.M.S. Barrosa was converted in H.M. Dockyard, Devonport to a Radar Picket Destroyer and she served in this role from 1962 until 1968.

Blazon: Red; A basilisk statant god.

Motto: Noli Irritare. (Do Not Irritate Me.)

Date: 4.7.1929   **Frame:** Shield

Herald: C. ffoulkes

Derivation of Name:
For the purpose of the badge design, it was assumed that the origination of this name was from Greek Mythology.* The basilisk was an awesome creature, reputed to possess the power of killing by means of its deadly glance and its burning, poisonous breath. According to Pliny, it was so called from a spot on its head that resembled a diadem. Medieval authors furnished it with 'a certain Combe or Coronet'. It was believed that if this creature was speared by a horseman, its poison passed through the weapon, killing both horse and rider. Although it was reputed to be only six inches in height, this creature was referred to as 'the King of the Serpents'.

Derivation of Badge:
The badge shows a cockatrice, (which is another mythical creature, synonymous with the basilisk), depicted in a traditional style. The basilisk is more frequently depicted in Heraldry as in the design, but drawn with the tail terminating in the form of a dragon's head. Even taking this variation into account, the badge is a straightforward illustration of the name.

Badge Heritage:
1. A 'B' Class Fleet Destroyer, built by J. Brown Ltd, launched in 1930 and lost as a result of damage received after being struck by bombs off Dunkirk whilst evacuating troops from the beaches on the 1st of June 1940.
2. A Royal Australian Navy shore establishment at Port Moresby, commissioned in 1943. The R.A.N. now have full title to the name of Basilisk.

Notes:
*It cannot be definitely confirmed that the first use of this name in 1695 was derived from the mythical beast. In the 15th Century, a basilisk was also a large brass cannon, capable of firing a ball up to 200 lbs. in weight. This type of weapon is mentioned by name in Shakespeare's 'Henry V' and was used at the Great Siege of Malta, which began in May 1565.

MPL Neg. No. 1876   April 1937

Blazon: Blue; A bassett hound proper, statant in fess upon a base representing grass also proper.

Motto: Good Hunting.

Date: 5.3.1935   **Frame:** Diamond

Herald: C. ffoulkes

Derivation of Name:
A bassett is a species of dog commonly used for hunting. Possessing a very good sense of smell, they are both persistent and obstinate. One of the oldest breeds of sporting dog in England, they were originally used for unearthing badgers and foxes. The name was selected in 1934 for the first ship of a class of Anti-Submarine Trawlers that were all to be named after breeds of dog.

Derivation of Badge:
This badge design is straightforward and needs no explanation. Mr. ffoulkes did not resort to 'art' designs for badges he submitted for approval very often, because he preferred to use Heraldic art, but in this instance it is difficult to see what alternative design could have been drawn.

Badge Heritage:
1. A 'Bassett' Class Anti-Submarine Trawler, built by Robb, launched in 1935 and sold for civilian use in 1948.

Notes:
The motto, whilst referring to the name, also denotes the role of the ship.

Only two ships of the class were built for the Royal Navy, (the other being H.M.S. Mastiff), but the design was so successful that the two hundred and fifty Trawlers that followed her over the next 10 years, deviated only in minor details from the original design.

Blazon: Barry wavy of six white and blue; Issuant from base and shown in plan a semi-circular fortification armed with a trucked cannon palewise all proper.

Motto: Not recorded.

Date: 10.2.1961   **Frame:** Standard

Herald: M. R. Trappes-Lomax

Derivation of Name:
A bastion is a defensive fortification which protrudes from the rampart, permitting flanking fire to be directed upon the attacker. Bastions were 'faced' and consisted of two flanks which served to protect the neighbouring bastions and two faces which met at an angle towards the enemy, thereby commanding a complete field of fire over the outworks and the ground in front.

Derivation of Badge:
The badge shows a plan view of a circular fortification, armed to seaward with a cannon. The design illustrates the name directly and needs no further explanation.

Badge Heritage:
1. A Tank Landing Craft, formerly LCT 4040, built by Arrol, launched in 1944 and named in 1956. She was sold to the Zambian Government in 1966.

Notes:
This ship, along with several others of her type, were named after defensive military fortifications, but not all of them were granted badges.

Blazon: Blue; A battleaxe gold.

Motto: Not recorded.

Date: 27.6.1945　　　**Frame:** Standard

Herald: Sir A. Cochrane

Derivation of Name:
The battleaxe was a weapon of war, in use from primitive times down to the era of gunpowder. It consisted of a blade, varying in shape and with one or more cutting edges, which was attached to a haft of varying length. Both single and double-handed versions were used and the exact form that the weapon took depended upon the period of history and the century in which it was made. Examples with two cutting edges are known to exist and in expert hands, this weapon was capable of inflicting fearsome injuries upon the victim. History records that a strong foot soldier could, (and did), cleave an unhorsed knight in armour clean through with a single blow!

Derivation of Badge:
The badge shows a Francisca battleaxe, commonly used in the Middle Ages, depicted gold on a blue field.

The design gives a very clear example of an illustration of the name.

Badge Heritage:
1. A 'Weapon' Class Fleet Destroyer, built by Yarrow, launched in 1945 and sold for scrapping in 1964.
2. A Type 22 Frigate, built by Yarrow and launched in 1977.

Notes:
The first ship to wear this badge was also the first ship of a class of Fleet Destroyers, all named after weapons, to be completed post-war. 19 of the class were originally ordered, but only 4 were completed, the remainder being cancelled or scrapped incomplete.

In 1957, the first ship to wear this badge was converted at H.M. Dockyard, Rosyth, to a Radar Picket Destroyer. She served in this role from 1959 until 1962, when she was damaged beyond repair following a collision with H.M.S. Ursa.

A Landing Ship (Dock) supplied under Lend-Lease in 1943 was scheduled to be named H.M.S. Battleaxe, but this did not take place and she joined the Fleet as H.M.S. Eastway.

W & L　　　　　　　　　　　　　　　　　　　　July 1953

W & L　　　　　　　　　　　　　　　　　　　　May 1987

Blazon: Blue; A thonged flanged mace bendwise sinister and a battleaxe in saltire all gold.

Motto: Not recorded.

Date: 12.6.1943   **Frame:** Standard

Herald: Sir A. Cochrane

Derivation of Name:
A battler is a fighter or warrior skilled in combat. The word is derived from the Medieval English word, 'batelur'.

Derivation of Badge:
The badge shows a medieval double-handed battleaxe crossed with another duel-purpose weapon, the flanged mace. They are both presented Heraldically and the design refers to a period of our history, when an individual's prowess at arms was greatly prized. The design also refers to the medieval origin of the name.

Badge Heritage:
1. An 'Attacker' Class Escort Carrier, formerly the *U.S.S. Altamaha*, built by Ingalls Shipbuilding and launched in 1942. She was transferred to the R.N. on 'Lend-Lease' and was returned to the U.S.N. in 1946.
2. A Tank Landing Ship, formerly LST 3015, built by Barclay Curle, launched in 1945, named in 1947 and sold for civilian use in 1956.

Notes:
39 of these 'Lend-Lease' Carriers served in the Royal Navy during the Second World War and performed sterling service. Only two were lost, H.M.S. Avenger, H.M.S. Dasher (by accident) and one other, H.M.S. Nabob, was damaged beyond repair.

MOD(N)   1942

G. Read Collection   7th September 1946

Blazon: Black; Two barrulets wavy in base white, the upper surmounted by a lighthouse also white, with lantern and rays gold.

Motto: Not recorded.

Date: 12.12.1946   **Frame:** Standard

Herald: Sir A. Cochrane

Derivation of Name:
Beachy Head is a promontory on the Sussex coast between Eastbourne and Seaford, forming the termination of the South Downs. The name is said to have been derived from the French 'Beau chef', which means 'beautiful head'. The Belle Tout lighthouse erected on the headland in 1831 was replaced in 1902 by the present light, erected at the foot of the cliffs.

On the 30th of June 1690, the Battle of Beachy Head was fought off the coast here, when a combined English and Dutch fleet was defeated by a French one. The name was selected in 1943 for one of a class of Repair Ships, all named after prominent headlands of the United Kingdom.

Derivation of Badge:
The badge design illustrates the present lighthouse at Beachy Head, shown arising out of the waves. It is thought that the black field depicts the night, thus allowing the beams of light to be shown and also to make reference to the fact that the main use of lighthouses is to warn mariners of coastal hazards during the hours of darkness.

There could also be some reference to the battle of Beachy Head by the use of this colour, as it was certainly a 'black day' for the Royal Navy.

Badge Heritage:
1. A Repair Ship, built by Burrard, launched in 1944 and transferred to the Royal Canadian Navy as *H.M.C.S. Cape Scott* in 1954. She served in the Royal Netherlands Navy as the *Vulkaan*, between 1946 and 1949.

Notes:
Earl Torrington, who commanded the English Fleet during the Battle of Beachy Head, was subsequently court-martialled on a charge of dereliction of duty and, although he was acquitted, he was not further employed.

MPL neg. No.3362   April 1950

14 H.M.S. BEAGLE (1804)

Blazon: Green; A beagle hound statant proper.

Motto: To A Finish.

Date: 6.1.1930   **Frame:** Shield

Herald: C. ffoulkes

Derivation of Name:
The beagle is the smallest species of dog used for hunting in Great Britain and they are normally used with foot beagle hunts, whose quarry is the hare. This breed can be traced back to the 15th Century, when diminutive fox-beagles were kept. They possess an extraordinarily keen scent, an acute intelligence and an incredible perseverance.

Derivation of Badge:
The use of green for the field of this badge is thought to denote the countryside, as green is often used in Heraldry for this purpose; however, the term 'beagle green' is common within hunting circles and is used to define the green colour of the uniform coat usually worn by beagle hunts. The dog is depicted in his natural colours and the complete design is an illustration of the name.

Badge Heritage:
1. A 'B' Class Fleet Destroyer, built by J. Brown Ltd, launched in 1930 and sold for scrapping in 1946.
2. A Survey Ship, built by Brooke Marine and launched in 1967.

Notes:
The motto denotes the perseverence of the beagle.

The third ship of this name was the famous sloop in which Charles Darwin made his well-known voyage (1831-1836).

It is of interest to record that the unofficial badge worn by the Destroyer of this name that served between 1910 and 1921 had a very similar design, and possibly influenced the design of the official one.

MPL Neg. No.1877   July 1935

W & L   May 1974

Blazon: Blue; A bee-hive beset with nine bees in orle volant fesswards all gold.

Motto: Not recorded.

Date: 23.6.1938   **Frame:** Circular

Herald: Sir A. Cochrane

Derivation of Name:
This name was selected in 1937 for one of the King George V Class Battleships then ordered, to commemorate Admiral of the Fleet Sir David Beatty (1871-1936). A very controversial officer, his meteoric rise to Flag rank under Royal patronage surprised many of his contemporaries. He commanded the Battle Cruiser Squadron of the Grand Fleet during the Battle of Jutland, fought on the 31st of May 1916.

In December 1916, he assumed command of the Grand Fleet on the retirement of Admiral Sir John Jellicoe and he was raised to the peerage on the 27th September 1919, with the titles of Earl Beatty, Viscount Borodale and Baron Beatty.

Derivation of Badge:
Both the field colour and the design of this badge are derived from the Arms of Earl Beatty which gave an example of 'canting' Arms, i.e., a pun on his name.

Badge Heritage:
This design was not used and for an explanation, please see Notes.

Notes:
It was very quickly appreciated that the adoption of this name would cause a major furore within Naval circles and the ship was re-named, prior to her launch, as H.M.S. Howe.

As a point of interest, many badge designs have a direct reference to prominent Naval officers of this century, but research has, so far, revealed that only one, (Admiral Sir J. D. Kelly), has been honoured by having a warship named after him.

Real Photos Neg. No.N1017   H.M.S. Howe October 1942

Blazon: Green; A pair of dividers extended gold, between the points a mariner's compass proper.

Motto: Weatherwise.

Date: 9.5.1920   **Frame:** Diamond

Herald: C. ffoulkes

Derivation of Name:
This name commemorates Rear Admiral Sir Francis Beaufort (1774-1857). He entered the Royal Navy in 1787 and was promoted to Commander in 1800. In 1805 he devised a scale of numbers for recording wind velocity and this scale, still in use today, is known as the Beaufort Scale. He was promoted to Captain in 1810 and served as the Hydrographer to the Admiralty from 1832 to 1855.

Derivation of Badge:
The design shows on a green* field, two of the main nautical navigation aids in use at the time that Admiral Beaufort was Hydrographer to the Admiralty. Within the guidelines laid down by Charles ffoulkes, this badge is alluding both to the derivation of the name and to the role of the ship.

Badge Heritage:
1. A Survey Ship (formerly a Fleet Minesweeper) built by Ailsa Shipbuilders Ltd, launched in 1919 and sold for scrapping in 1938.

Notes:
The motto is a direct reference to Sir Francis Beaufort's invention.
  * The use of green as a field colour for a badge design concerned with the work of the Hydrographic Department, is at first difficult to understand, until it is realised that the shade of green used is described as 'sea-green'.

MPL Neg. No.2502   May 1937

Blazon: Blue; A portcullis chained all gold, within a horseshoe inverted white.

Motto: Not recorded.

Date: 12.12.1941   **Frame:** Standard

Herald: Sir A. Cochrane

Derivation of Name:
When the Ship's Names Committee allocated this name to one of the 'Hunt' Class Escort Vessels ordered in 1939, the derivation was of Genealogical origin. Beaufort is the family name of the descendants of John O'Gaunt, Duke of Lancaster, owners of the Beaufort hunt that covers parts of Gloucestershire, Somerset and Wiltshire, whose full title is "The Duke of Beaufort's". This foxhound hunt was founded in 1786 by the 5th Duke of Beaufort and his successors have held the Mastership since that time, except during 1898 and 1899.

Derivation of Badge:
As a new derivation was applicable to this name, the existing badge described in the previous entry was no longer appropriate and a new design was produced. The blue field depicts the colour of the hunt uniform, whilst the gold portcullis is derived from the Crest of the Beaufort family. The white horseshoe alludes to the sport of hunting from horseback.

Badge Heritage:
1. A 'Hunt' Class Type II Escort Vessel, built by Cammell Laird, launched in 1941 and transferred to the Royal Norwegian Navy in 1952.

Notes:
This is not the only example of a badge being changed due to a new derivation or classification of the name, as will be seen later in this work.

Blazon: Blue; A cinquefoil white, charged with a strawberry leaf proper.

Motto: Not recorded.

Date: 12.12.1946   **Frame:** Standard

Herald: Sir A. Cochrane

Derivation of Name:
Beauly Firth is a stretch of water to the west of Inverness, Invernesshire. The word 'firth' means a narrow inlet of the sea or the estuary of a river. This name was selected in 1943 for one of a class of Repair Ships all named after stretches of sheltered water on the Scottish coast.

Derivation of Badge:
The land surrounding Beauly Firth has long been the property of the Fraser family. Lovat Castle, which formerly stood on the bank of the Firth, was given to Hugh Fraser, Lord of Lovat, by King James VI in 1367, but this family can be traced back to 1160.

The Arms of the family of Fraser bear white cinquefoils on a blue field. One use for this charge in Heraldry is to depict strawberry flowers, and another name for it is 'fraise', (the French for 'strawberry'.) The Fraser family were granted fraises as a pun upon their name and a strawberry leaf, in its proper form, has been added to the badge design, emphasising that the cinquefoil is intended to represent a strawberry flower, thus confirming the connection between the name of the ship and the Fraser family.

Badge Heritage:
1. A Maintenance Ship for hull repairs built by Redhead Ltd, launched in 1944 and sold for civilian use in 1948.

Notes:
Of the seven ships of this class, only H.MS. Beauly Firth and H.M.S. Holm Sound were granted badges.

8th December 1945

Blazon: Blue; A round demi-tower embattled white, masoned proper, floatant diversely from its flagstaff also white, a pennon per fess gold, and red.

Motto: Not recorded.

Date: 18.11.1941   **Frame:** Standard

Herald: Sir A. Cochrane

Derivation of Name:
Beaumaris, (which means 'fair marsh'), is a town in Anglesey on Beaumaris Bay. The dominant feature of this town is its famous moated castle with twelve round towers and within its walls a small dock. The castle, founded by Edward I in 1295, but never completed, formed part of a long chain of fortifications built to keep the Welsh under control.

Derivation of Badge:
The badge is derived from part of the ancient Seal of the Town, as Beaumaris did not have a grant of Arms. The tower, which is in reference to the castle of Beaumaris, is shown flying a gold and red pennon. These colours are the livery colours of Edward I and have been used to denote that the castle was founded by him. The badge therefore denotes both the town and the founder of its castle.

Badge Heritage:
1. A 'Bangor' Class Fleet Minesweeper, built by Ailsa Shipbuilding, launched in 1940 and sold for scrapping in 1948.

Notes:
Sir Arthur Cochrane designed all the badges for this class of warship, with most badges being derived from the Arms of the town.

MPL Neg. No.2628

1941

Blazon: White; A beaver sejant proper, grasping in its forepaws a trident inverted to dexter base gold.

Motto: Not recorded.

Date: 21.6.1968   **Frame:** Standard

Herald: Sir W. Verco

Derivation of Name:
A beaver is a rodent of the Castor genus. Very industrious animals, they are noted for their intelligence.

Derivation of Badge:
The badge shows a very aggressive beaver poised to strike downwards with a trident. This weapon is often used in Naval Heraldry to denote maritime seapower and also (as in this case), seaborne weaponry.

The design of this badge is a direct reference both to the derivation of the name and also to the role of the Anti-Submarine Frigate for which the badge was designed. The field colour was chosen in this instance solely to provide contrast for the design.

Badge Heritage:
1. A Type 22 Frigate, built by Yarrow, launched in 1982 and accepted into service in 1984.

Notes:
There is a remarkable similarity between the beaver in this badge and the unofficial one worn by the Destroyer of the same name that served from 1912 until 1921, when it is considered that the Heraldic artist who painted the modern design had no knowledge of the earlier one.

As a point of interest, when various designs were being considered for this badge in 1968, one showed a top hat, denoting another meaning of the name 'beaver'!

Navpic

Blazon: White; A swan with wings addorsed black, statant within a horseshoe inverted red, all inclined to profile.

Motto: Not recorded.

Date: 18.12.1941   **Frame:** Standard

Herald: Sir A. Cochrane

Derivation of Name:
Bedale is a market town in the North Riding of Yorkshire, from which the local foxhunt derives its name. The Bedale country once formed a part of the immense Raby hunt territory.

This name was first selected in 1939 for one of the 'Hunt' Class Escort Vessels ordered in that year.

Derivation of Badge:
The white field of the badge is thought to denote the colour of the Yorkshire rose.

The horseshoe denotes the sport of hunting on horseback and is coloured red to illustrate the hunt uniform worn by the riders of the Bedale Hunt, which is a red jacket with a black collar. The black swan records the fact that the inaugural meeting of the hunt was held on the 31st of October 1816 at a public house in Bedale called the 'Black Swan'!

Badge Heritage:
1. A 'Hunt' Class Type II Escort Vessel, built by Hawthorn Leslie, launched in 1941 and sold for scrapping in 1959.

Notes:
On completion, H.M.S. Bedale was transferred to the Polish Navy, and served with them from 1942 until 1946 as the *Slazak*. She was transferred in 1953 to the Indian Navy as the *Godavari*.

MPL Neg. No.1990 (Slazak)   1943

Blazon: Blue; A sheathed Bedouin jambiya the scabbard gold, hilt and crampet silver.

Motto: Honour and Chivalry.

Date: 13.10.1937   **Frame:** Shield

Herald: Sir A. Cochrane

Derivation of Name:
The name 'Bedouin' is derived from the Arabic word 'badw', which means desert, hence 'dwellers in the desert'. The Bedouin are a race or tribe of nomadic Arabs and were once notorious plunderers of caravans and travellers.

Fiercely independent, they regarded all foreigners as trespassers. However, they invariably respected a safe conduct pass and these could be purchased from a sheikh of the tribe. The proverbial Arab hospitality was then freely extended and their word, once given, was not broken. Some aspects of their code of conduct were alien to European eyes, but by Arabic standards they were considered to be an honorable and chivalrous people.

Derivation of Badge:
This is a very simple and effective design, showing a sheathed Bedouin dagger. The intricate workmanship of the weapon has been faithfully reproduced.

The fact that the weapon is sheathed is significant, as in Heraldry, a sheathed weapon is used to indicate that there is no hostile intent.

Badge Heritage:
1. A 'Tribal' Class Destroyer, built by Denny, launched in 1937 and lost on the 15th of June 1942, under the command of Cdr. B. G. Scurfield, when she was torpedoed by an Italian aircraft during Operation 'Harpoon', (a convoy to Malta), following damage received from gunfire of two Italian cruisers. Twenty-eight ratings were lost.

Notes:
The motto, whilst making reference to the conduct of the Bedouin towards their allies, was a good example for the ship's company.

Although this name dates back to 1914, the first was a hired trawler that served with her civilian name unchanged.

MPL Neg. No.1964   May 1939

Blazon: Blue; A bee-hive beset with four bees one two and one all gold.

Motto: Ex Industria Honor. (By Industry Honour.)

Date: 14.2.1924   **Frame:** Diamond

Herald: C. ffoulkes

Derivation of Name:
The bee is one of a group of sting-bearing insects of the order Hymenoptera. This 'small ship' name was given in 1914 to one of a class of River Gunboats, all named after insects.

Derivation of Badge:
The badge shows a bee-hive with four bees presented in Heraldic fashion. All eleven ships of the 'Insect' Class River Gunboats, were given badges. This is the only one that shows more than one of the insect in the designs, where an insect has been used to illustrate the name. It was not possible to depict a single bee for this badge, as the design for another ship, (H.M.S. Wanderer), shows a single bee. This design places four bees in their natural environment and also shows the hive, to which they will return after their labours.

Badge Heritage:
1. An 'Insect' Class River Gunboat, built by Ailsa Shipbuilding, launched in 1915 and sold for scrapping in 1939.
2. A Coastal Forces Base at Weymouth from 1942 to 1943.
3. A Coastal Forces Base at Holyhead from 1943 to 1945.

Notes:
Bees have long been used in Heraldry to convey or depict industriousness and the motto refers to this fact.

The choice of this name in 1941 for use by the Coastal Forces Base at Weymouth was very apt, as most Coastal Forces Bases were named after insects with stings in their tails. The reason for this will be explained in a later volume that will include the 'Type' Badges for Motor Torpedo Boats and Fast Patrol Craft.

Blazon: Blue; An Indian cobra coiled its head reared in readiness to strike gold.

Motto: Rise and Strike.

Date: 28.3.1944   **Frame:** Standard

Herald: Sir A. Cochrane

Derivation of Name:
The word 'begum' is of Indian origin and is used as a title to denote a Queen, or a lady of high rank, in Hindustan, but the use of this title is also common throughout the Indian continent.

The name was first selected in 1942 for one of a class of Escort Carriers, known as the 'Ruler' Class, named after 'rulers of men'.

Derivation of Badge:
This design was suggested by the ship's officers in 1943. The snake clearly shows the origin of the name by the 'spectacle' markings on its head. These are peculiar to the Indian cobra, (called locally the 'Naja Naja'), which gives a warning that it may be about to strike by rearing its head and spreading its hood. The cobra, depicted gold to allude to royalty, is shown in this aggressive posture.

Badge Heritage:
1. A 'Ruler' Class Escort Carrier, formerly the *U.S.S. Balinas*, built by Seattle Shipbuilding, launched in 1942, transferred to the Royal Navy on 'Lend-Lease' in 1943 and was returned to the U.S. Navy in 1946.

Notes:
The motto, whilst referring to the design of the badge, also denotes the offensive capability of the ship's aircraft.

W & L   1942

Blazon: Blue; Upon three barrulets wavy in base white, a seahorse green, langued red, gorged with a mural crown gold.

Motto: Pro Tanto Quid Retribuamus. (We Give As Good As We Get.)*

Date: 18.3.1937   **Frame:** Pentagon

Herald: Sir A. Cochrane

Derivation of Name:
This name honours the City of Belfast, Northern Ireland. The city has enjoyed a long connection with the Royal Navy and in its harbour were three very large ship-building yards, including that of Messrs. Harland & Wolff, the builders of this warship.

The name was first selected in 1936 for one of the two 'Modified Town' Class Cruisers ordered in that year.

Derivation of Badge:
The design has been derived from the Arms of the City. These Arms include a seahorse as its crest and two seahorses as its Supporters, but it is the Crest that has been adapted to provide the badge.

Badge Heritage:
1. A 'Modified Town' Class Cruiser, built by Harland & Wolff, launched in 1938 and preserved as a museum-ship in the Pool of London.** This ship's wartime career included being severely damaged on the 21st of November, 1939, by a mine that broke her back and put her out of action for 26 months. She was also in Scapa Flow the night H.M.S. Royal Oak was torpedoed by U-47 and could have suffered the same fate.

    The last time her guns were fired 'in anger' was during the Korean War in 1952.

Notes:
* There is no motto shown for this ship in the Ship's Badges Committee's records, but the writer's father, who was a Chief Ordnance Artificer in her from 1945 until 1947, still has records of her service during this period, which include the motto as given above.

** This fine ship, which is now the responsibility of the Imperial War Museum, has on board a very interesting collection of ship's badges, boat's badges and tompions, both official and unofficial. A visit to this warship is highly recommended.

A. J. Wilkinson   October 1945

Blazon: Barry wavy of ten white and blue;
A demi-griffin erazed gold, armed and langued red.

Motto: Not recorded.

Date: 3.3.1953   **Frame:** Standard

Herald: Sir A. Cochrane

Derivation of Name:
This name is from Greek Mythology. Bellerophon was the son of the Corinthian King Glaucus and Eurymede and was originally named Hipponous. As a youth he was able to tame the immortal horse Pegasus with the aid of a golden bridle given to him by Athene. When he later accidently killed the Corinthian, Belerus, he was named Bellerophon. (This name means, 'bearing darts, or killer of Belerus'.) As a punishment he was exiled first to Argos and then to Lycia, where King Iobates gave him a number of dangerous tasks from which he was not expected to return alive.

With the help of Pegasus, he accomplished his missions and by his marriage to King Iobates' daughter, Philone, he succeeded to the throne of Lycia.

Derivation of Badge:
The design of this badge commemorates the service of the first ship of this name at the Battle of Trafalgar on the 21st of October 1805. At the commencement of that action, her commanding officer, Capt. J. Cooke, was killed and Lieut. William Pyrce Cumby assumed command, fighting the ship until she was dismasted. By the marriage of the daughter of his youngest son to Canon Henry Spurrier, the family of Cumby was conjoined with that of Spurrier, whose arms include a golden griffin on a blue field. The field of barry wavy is a simple reference to the sea and may allude to the anchorage of the Reserve Fleet at Portsmouth.

Badge Heritage:
1. Reserve Fleet, Portsmouth from 1950 until 1971.

Notes:
As can be seen from the photographs, many ships comprised the Reserve Fleet at one time, each with their own badge, but this badge was granted for the use by the administration establishment.

D. Maxted   August 1952

R. H. Osbourne Collection   1956

Skyfotos   1959

Blazon: Blue; A trophy of classic weapons surmounted by an oval shield ensigned by a crested helmet all gold.

Motto: Not recorded.

Date: 7.7.1943   **Frame:** Standard

Herald: Sir A. Cochrane

Derivation of Name:
This is a prize-name, formerly the French *'Bellone'*, captured in 1747 and re-named H.M.S. Bellona.

'Bellone' is the French name for Bellona, the Roman goddess of war. According to some interpretations, she was the sister of Mars, the god of war; according to others, she was his wife. Her temple, in the Campus Martius at Rome, was founded in 296 B.C. It was here that the Senators gave audiences to foreign ambassadors and Roman generals returning from the wars. At its entrance stood a small column, known as the 'Column of War', against which a spear was thrown to indicate a declaration of war.

Derivation of Badge:
The badge shows a trophy of arms, depicted gold, denoting warfare rather than the goddess of war herself. If one examines carefully the helmet in the design, it can be seen that the badge is giving a very clever reference to the origin of this name in the Royal Navy, as this helmet is that of a French Dragoon, circa 1750.

Badge Heritage:
1. A 'Modified Dido' Class Cruiser, built by Fairfield, launched in 1942 and sold for scrapping in 1959.
    This ship was on loan to the Royal New Zealand Navy between 1948 and 1956.

Notes:
This is another example where the derivation of the name has been skilfully 'hidden' in the design.

Blazon: Blue; A bell white, charged with a hurt, thereon a mullet also white.

Motto: Not recorded.

Date: 1.10.1941   **Frame:** Standard

Herald: Sir A. Cochrane

Derivation of Name:
This name was first used in the Royal Navy during the First World War, when a hired trawler served in her civilian name. In 1940 it was revived for one of the fifty destroyers transferred to the Royal Navy from the United States. These ships, known in the Royal Navy as the 'Town' class, were all said to be named after towns common to both Great Britain and the United States. It is thought that this name honours Belmont, Lancashire, but due to the number of towns in the United States of this name, it is not possible to state with certainty, the town honoured.*

Derivation of Badge:
The badge shows a church bell with a star on a blue background placed upon it. The design is an example of 'canting', or punning arms, i.e. a bell surmounted by a star – a 'bell-mont'. The star denotes the American origin of the ship because this device has been the military emblem of the United States since the First World War.

Badge Heritage:
1. A 'Town' Class Destroyer, formerly the *U.S.S.Satterlee*, built by Newport News, launched in 1918 and named H.M.S. Belmont in 1940. On the 31st of January 1942, as part of the escort for Convoy NA2, whilst under the command of Lieut.-Cdr. G. B. Harding R.N., she was torpedoed by *U-82* and sunk with all hands. Eight officers and one hundred and thirty ratings were lost.

Notes:
The writers are presently undertaking additional research into various questions posed by the badges for this class of ship. It is not thought that the intention of giving this class of ships names common to both countries, was to honour one particular town in each country, due to the numerous examples of several towns of the same name in both Great Britain and the United States. It may well be that the idea was to promote as many Anglo-American ties as possible. The transfer of these ships to the Royal Navy was symbolic and although their fighting value was questionable**, they were a very solid gesture on the part of the United States to support us at a time when our fortunes in the war were at a very low ebb. *In 1949, thirty-nine badges of the ships of this class were despatched from H.M.Dockyard, Chatham, to the British Joint Services Mission, Washington D.C. and the Admiralty Delegation, New York City, for presentation to the various towns in the United States subsequently considered to have been honoured by the adoption of their name by the Royal Navy. Ascertaining the actual towns is one of our areas of research. **In spite of the severe problems encountered in maintaining these ships, the class as a whole still managed to destroy 11 U-Boats.

WSPL Brownell Collection   circa 1941

Blazon: White; The head of a peacock erazed proper, enfiled by a ducal coronet gold.

Motto: Not recorded.

Date: 4.6.1942   **Frame:** Standard

Herald: Sir A. Cochrane

Derivation of Name:
Belvoir is a village to the west of Grantham, Lincolnshire that has given its name to a foxhunt covering parts of the border area between Lincolnshire and Leicestershire. The name was first used by the Royal Navy for one of the 'Hunt' Class Fleet Minesweepers and selected again in 1940 for one of the 'Hunt' Class Escort Vessels.

Derivation of Badge:
The colour white for the field is thought to have been used solely to provide contrast for the very colourful peacock's head placed upon it. The head itself is derived from the Crest of the Manners family with the addition of a ducal coronet to illustrate the family title, the Dukes of Rutland. This family held Mastership of the hunt almost continuously from 1750 until 1896.

Badge Heritage:
1. A 'Hunt' Class Type III Escort Vessel, built by Cammell Laird, launched in 1941 and sold for scrapping in 1957.

Notes:
Sir Arthur Cochrane designed all the badges for the 'Hunt' Class Escort Vessels that were granted them — a total of 79. This badge is one of the 15 that does not bear a direct visual reference to the sport of hunting.

MOD(N)   29th May 1945

Blazon: Black: A harpy statant guardant its head wreathed with a garland of flowers all gold.

Motto: Usque Ad Finem. (To The Very End).

Date: 3.5.1920   **Frame:** Circular

Herald: C. ffoulkes

Derivation of Name:
This name commemorates Vice-Admiral John Benbow, (1653-1702), whose final action was a source of great inspiration at the time. On the 19th of August 1702, whilst commanding a squadron based at Jamaica, he attacked a force of French ships under the command of Commodore Du Casse.

Although Admiral Benbow was deserted by some of his captains,* he carried on a running fight, almost single-handed, for five days. His leg was taken off by a chain-shot during the battle and he also suffered a head-wound.

Nevertheless he continued to conduct the action from a cradle on his quarter-deck, until the disabled condition of his flag-ship, H.M.S. Breda, forced him to abandon the chase and return to Jamaica, where he died from his wounds on the 4th of November 1702.

Derivation of Badge:
The black field of the badge mourns the death of Admiral Benbow, whilst the gold harpy with its wreath of flowers is the Crest of the Benbow family.

Badge Heritage:
1. An 'Iron Duke' Class Battleship, built by Beardmore, launched in 1913 and sold for scrapping in 1931.
2. A shore Establishment at Trinidad, West Indies, from 1941 to 1947.

Notes:
This badge is very similar to the unofficial one worn by the previous ship of the name, also a Battleship, that served from 1890 until 1909.

The motto acknowledges the tenacity of Admiral Benbow.

*Admiral Benbow's squadron consisted of H.M.S. Defiance (Capt. Kirkley), H.M.S. Pendennis (Capt. Hudson), H.M.S. Windsor (Capt. Constable), H.M.S. Breda (Flag) (Capt. Fogg), H.M.S. Greenwich (Capt. Wade), H.M.S. Ruby (Capt. Walton) and H.M.S. Falmouth (Capt. Vincent). On the 6th of October 1702, all of these Captains were tried by court-martial for the unparalleled act of deserting a British Admiral in the face of an enemy fleet. Captain Vincent and Captain Fogg were convicted of having signed a document to the effect that they would not serve under Admiral Benbow's command, but as they had behaved gallantly in action, they were temporarily suspended from rank and pay. Captain Walton had also joined this consipiracy, but renounced it afterwards and fought with courage until his ship was disabled. Captains Kirkley and Wade were sentenced to death and shot at Plymouth on the deck of H.M.S. Bristol by Royal Marines. Captain Constable was cashiered and sentenced to be imprisoned during the pleasure of Her Majesty Queen Anne. Captain Hudson had died some days before the trial, otherwise there is little doubt that he too would have been shot.

Blazon: Gold; A triangle purple, charged with a sprig of white heather proper.

Motto: Not recorded.

Date: 30.6.1949   **Frame:** Standard

Herald: Sir A. Cochrane

Derivation of Name:
Ben Lomond is a mountain on the eastern shore of Loch Lomond in Stirlingshire, Scotland. This very scenic mountain is covered with vegetation almost to its 3,192 ft. peak and an extensive view is obtained from the summit. It is terminated on its northern side by a precipice of 2,000 ft. This name was first selected in 1947 for one of the two LST(Q) ships converted to serve in experimental roles;* both were named after Scottish mountains.

Derivation of Badge:
The gold field of the badge denotes the location of the mountain, as the Arms and Flag of Scotland display a yellow field. A mountain or peak is indicated on O.S. maps with a triangular symbol. In the badge this symbol is coloured purple to indicate the purple heather that grows in profusion on the slopes of the mountain in season. White heather, being a hybrid, can be found, if one is lucky enough, growing amongst the common heath. In recent times, white heather has become almost as symbolic as the thistle as an emblem of Scotland and a sprig of this plant has been placed on the triangle in the badge.

Badge Heritage:
1. A Landing Ship Tank, (LST3013), converted to an L.S.T.(Q), built by H & W, launched in 1945 and named in 1947. She served as an experimental ship and was engaged at one time in N.B.C. trials. She was sold for scrapping in 1960.

Notes:
* The other was H.M.S. Ben Nevis, but she was not given a badge.

Blazon: Gold; A torteau, charged with two hunting horns in saltire gold, surmounted by a cross patee white.

Motto: Dieu Avec Nous. (God With Us.)

Date: 20.2.1940   **Frame:** Diamond

Herald: Sir A. Cochrane

Derivation of Name:
The historic family of Berkeley have hunted large tracts of Southern England since the second half of the 16th Century. In 1807, Colonel William Berkeley established a pack of foxhounds at the family seat in Gloucestershire and the Mastership has remained in the family ever since.

This hunt, whose full name is the "Earl of Berkeley", is very large and covers some 350 square miles of country. The name was selected in 1939 for one of the 'Hunt' Class Escort Vessels ordered in that year.

Derivation of Badge:
The gold field of the badge denotes the distinctive yellow coats of the hunt uniform. The red roundel with its white cross patee is derived from the Arms of Berkeley, which includes white crosses patee on a red field; the golden hunting horns are in direct reference to the sport of hunting.

Badge Heritage:
1. A 'Hunt' Class Type I Escort Vessel, built by Cammell Laird, launched in 1940 and sunk off Dieppe on the 19th of August 1942 by a depth charge from H.M.S. Albrighton, after receiving extensive damage from enemy bombing.*
2. A 'Hunt' Class Mine Counter Measures ship, built by Vosper-Thornycroft and launched in 1986.

Notes:
The motto of the ship is also that of the Berkeley family.

* A very well known photograph of this ship exists, taken at the moment of her scuttling by H.M.S. Albrighton and it is always mistakenly captioned to have been taken at the moment she was struck by bombs.

WSPL Brownell Collection   1940

Vosper Thorneycroft   July 1987

Blazon: Red; A round tower within an orle composed of ten crosses patee all white.

Motto: Not recorded.

Date: 15.4.1954   **Frame:** Standard

Herald: M. R. Trappes-Lomax

Derivation of Name:
Berkeley Castle, one of the noblest feudal castles in England, stands upon rising ground on the eastern shore of the River Severn in Gloucestershire. The Domesday Book records the tenure as belonging to one Roger de Berkeley, and this castle is remarkable for the fact that the Berkeley family, still holding its tenure, remain in residence.

Derivation of Badge:
This design is a direct reference to the Berkeley family and their castle. The red field and the ten white crosses are taken from the Arms of the Berkeleys, whilst the white castle is an Heraldic representation of the splendid 12th Century feudal stronghold, honoured by the name of this ship.

Badge Heritage:
1. A 'Castle' Class Corvette, built by Barclay Curle, launched in 1943 and sold for scrapping in 1956.

Notes:
For an explanation of the long interval of time between the launch of this ship and the grant of her badge, please see the Notes for H.M.S. Bamborough Castle.

As a gruesome historical footnote, Berkeley Castle was the scene of the murder of King Edward II in 1327, by henchmen of his wife, Queen Isabella of France.

Blazon: White; A demi-lion affrontee erazed red, armed and langued blue, supporting with its dexter paw a trident red.

Motto: Coeur De Lion. (Lionheart.)

Date: 8.6.1942   **Frame:** Standard

Herald: Sir A. Cochrane

Derivation of Name:
Bermuda is a former British Colony in the Atlantic Ocean, about 600 miles east by south from Cape Hatteras on the American coast. Its correct name is The Bermudas, as it is a group of about one hundred islands of which Bermuda is the largest. They derive their name from their Spanish discoverer, Juan Bermudez, who sighted them in 1515. According to his own account, the islands were discovered at some earlier date (than that of his own visit), and there is a map published in 1511, in Martyr's Legato Baby-lonica, which shows the islands in an approximately accurate position. In 1609, when Admiral George Somer's ship *Sea Venture* was wrecked on a reef off the islands, they were uninhabited. This reef is still known as the 'Sea Venture Flat'. Admiral Somers, who had escorted several other ships containing settlers, died the following year and these settlers, ignorant of the prior claims of Bermudez, named the islands Somers Islands and this name is still sometimes used.

Derivation of Badge:
In 1942 the Arms of Bermuda included: Argent, upon a mount green, a lion sejant affrontee red.

These Arms have been adapted for the design of the badge, the lion being given a red trident which in Naval Heraldry is normally used as symbolic of naval weaponry.

Badge Heritage:
1. A 'Colony' Class Cruiser, built by J. Brown Ltd., launched in 1941 and sold for scrapping in 1965.

Notes:
Facilities for the establishment and use of naval and air bases on the East coast of Bermuda, (the Great Bay), and other British Colonies were granted to the United States in 1940, in exchange for fifty former U.S. Navy destroyers. (See H.M.S. Belmont.)

W & L

August 1945

Blazon: Barry wavy of ten white and blue;
Two sprigs of bramble bowed and conjoined in base slipped leaved and fructed all proper.

Motto: Not recorded.

Date: 29.10.1946   **Frame:** Standard

Herald: Sir A. Cochrane

Derivation of Name:
Berry Head is a promontory on the Devonshire coast near Brixham, overlooking Tor Bay.

In the Iron Age, a local tribe built a fortification along this promontory and from this the name 'Berry Head' is derived as the word 'berry' is a corruption of 'byri' or 'byrig', the Saxon word for 'fortification'.

This name was selected in 1943 for one of a class of Repair Ships, all named after geographical features on the coastline of the United Kingdom.

Derivation of Badge:
The field colour of the badge denotes the sea, overlooked by the headland, whilst the two sprigs of bramble with their fruit, (berries), can be seen to be taken from the very top of a blackberry bush. Apart from the obvious meaning of the word 'head', another definition is "any rounded or compact part of a plant, usually at the top of the stem", therefore, this design yields literally, a 'berry head'.

Badge Heritage:
1. A Maintenance and Repair Ship, built by Burrard, launched in 1944 and sold for scrapping in 1987.

Notes:
At the time of her disposal, this ship was one of the very few still in service with the Royal Navy, built during the Second World War.

MPL Neg. No.3363

August 1950

Blazon: White; Issuant from a mount in base a wych-elm tree all proper, surmounting the trunk and statant upon the mount a bear black, collared and chained gold.

Motto: Victoriae Gloria Merces. (Glory Is The Reward For Victory.)

Date: 29.9.1924   **Frame:** Pentagon

Herald: C. ffoulkes

Derivation of Name:
Berwick, a town at the mouth of the River Tweed, was previously a County, as with Tweedmouth and Spittal, it formed 'a county of a borough and a town'. (It is now part of the County of Northumberland.*) The town has a turbulent history and during the border struggles between the 12th and 15th Centuries, it changed hands no fewer than thirteen times, before finally becoming English territory in 1482.

Derivation of Badge:
The design of this badge is derived from an early seal** of Berwick-upon-Tweed, as no Arms for Berwick existed in 1924. From the same seal, Berwick Borough Council adapted their present grant of Arms, matriculated in 1958.

Badge Heritage:
1. A 'County' Class Cruiser, built by Fairfield, launched in 1926 and sold for scrapping in 1948.
2. A 'Rothesay' Class Anti-Submarine Frigate, built by Harland & Wolff, launched in 1959 and sold for scrapping in 1986.

Notes:
The motto of the ship is a modification of the motto of the town.
    * The present County is in Scotland, but the first ship was one of a class of Cruisers all named after English Counties, whilst the second was one of a class all named after coastal towns of the United Kingdom.
    ** The use of the wych-elm and bear in the design is said to have been chosen to give a pun on the name of the town – 'bear-wych'.

MPL Neg. No.1241   February 1928

W & L   July 1979

Blazon: White; A beaver passant proper, charged with a hurt, thereon a mullet white.

Motto: Not recorded.

Date: 1.10.1941   **Frame:** Standard

Herald: Sir A. Cochrane

Derivation of Name:
The selection of this name in 1940, chosen for one of the fifty Destroyers transferred from the United States to the Royal Navy, honoured the town of Beverley in East Yorkshire and a city of the same name in Essex County, Massachusetts, U.S.A. These ships were said to have been named after towns and cities common to both countries.

Beverley, East Yorks., the county town of the East Ridings until 1974, is dominated by a magnificent minster, founded in 700 A.D. by the Archbishop of York, (later canonised as St. John of Beverley), and completed in the 13th Century.

Although it is ten miles from the sea, the town's shipyards on the River Hull once built fishing trawlers, (and also many small warships for the Royal Navy during the Second World War.)

Beverley, Mass. was settled in 1626 and it was here in 1775 at Glovers Wharf that the schooner *Hannah* was outfitted and commissioned by General George Washington as the first warship of the United States Navy.

Derivation of Badge:
This design is derived from the Seals of the town of Beverley, E. Yorks., recorded at the Visitation of Heralds 1584-5. These gave a pun on the meaning of the town's name, (according to one authority, derived from the Saxon 'Beverloga' – meaning 'the lake of beavers').

The beaver features a white star on a blue roundel, denoting the United States origin of the ship and the significance of this emblem is explained in the derivation of the badge for H.M.S. Belmont.

Badge Heritage:
1. A 'Town' Class Destroyer, formerly the *U.S.S. Branch*, built by Newport News, launched in 1919 and named in 1940. She was lost on the 11th of April 1943, whilst forming part of the escort for Convoy ON 176, when she was torpedoed by *U-188*. Nine officers, including her Captain, Lieut.Cdr. R. A. Price, R.N. and one hundred and thirty-nine ratings were lost.

Notes:
Not all of the fifty of this class of ship served in the Royal Navy, for several were transferred directly to the Royal Canadian Navy, some named after towns and cities common to Canada and the United States.

G. Read Collection

circa 1942

Blazon: Blue; A Bherunda bird displayed gold, fimbriated red.

Motto: Not recorded.

Date: 11.6.1945   **Frame:** Standard

Herald: Sir A. Cochrane

Derivation of Name:
This name is from Sinhalese Heraldry. Bherunda was the name of a bird, which was used as an Heraldic device displayed upon the banner flown by the ancient chiefs of an outlying district of the old Kandyan kingdom in Ceylon. Known as the Three Korales, it was situated about sixty miles to the east of Colombo. This mythical bird is very similar to the double-headed eagle of European Heraldry.

Derivation of Badge:
The badge shows the Bherunda bird taken from the banner of the Three Korales. This design was suggested by the Royal Naval Air Station at Colombo, Ceylon. Most Fleet Air Arm Stations were named after birds, both real and mythical. The use of this bird also locates the airfield for which the badge was designed.

Badge Heritage:
1. A Royal Naval Air Station at Colombo, Ceylon from 1943 until 1945.

Notes:
The writers had some hesitation before deciding to use the Heraldic term, 'fimbriated' red, in the blazon, as it places the colour red upon blue, thereby contravening an Heraldic convention that 'colour should not be placed upon another colour'. (Silver, [or white], and gold are termed 'metals' and also should not be placed one upon the other.) However, the sealed pattern of this badge shows that there is a well defined red framing surrounding the bird. It may well be that this colour was used to denote the field colour of the banner of the Three Korales.

We are extremely grateful to Mr. T. R. Blurton of the Department of Oriental Antiquities, The British Museum, for identifying this mythological bird, and also to Mr. Len Lovell of the Fleet Air Arm Museum for supplying an illustration of the airfield.

FAA Museum

Blazon: Red; A key with ward in chief gold, enfiled by a stirrup white.

Motto: Not recorded.

Date: 12.12.1941   **Frame:** Standard

Herald: Sir A. Cochrane

Derivation of Name:
Bicester, a market town in Oxfordshire, has given its name to the local foxhunt*. The town lies in the centre of the hunt country and the pack was founded in 1800 by Sir Thomas Mostyn, who retained Mastership for the next twenty-nine years. This name was originally used during the First World War for one of the 'Hunt' Class Fleet Minesweepers and was revived in 1940 for use by one of the 'Hunt' Class Escort Vessels.

Derivation of Badge:
The field colour of the badge refers to the red uniform coat of the huntsmen and a stirrup is included in the design to denote that the Bicester hunt is a mounted one; it also represents the class of the ship. Prior to the formation of the present hunt, a Mr John Warde hunted the area, and although this gentleman does not appear to be entitled to Arms, a key with its 'Ward' uppermost, has been used in the badge as a pun on his name, to record his very early connection with the hunt.

Badge Heritage:
1. A 'Hunt' Class Type II Escort Vessel, built by Hawthorn Leslie, launched in 1941 and sold for scrapping in 1956.
2. A Mine Counter Measures Vessel, built by Vosper-Thornycroft and launched in 1985.

Notes:
* In 1947, the hunt was amalgamated with the Warden Hill pack and given a new title: the 'Bicester and Warden Hill'.

In the same year, the first ship to wear this badge was re-classified as an Anti-Aircraft Frigate (along with several of her sisters).

MOD(N)   June 1942

Navpic   14th February 1986

Blazon: Blue; Issuant from four barrulets in base engrailed and invected to represent wavelets gold, and green, a triple-spanned arched bridge silver, beneath the centre span an ancient ship also silver.

Motto: Bide Your Time.

Date: 15.4.1930   **Frame:** Diamond

Herald: C. ffoulkes

Derivation of Name:
Bideford is a port and market town in North Devonshire, near Barnstaple. Straddling the River Torridge, the town is linked by a bridge, built in the 15th Century, nearly seven hundred feet long and constructed of twenty-four spans, all of different width. It was at Bideford that Kingsley wrote part of 'Westward Ho!'.

It was also the birthplace of Sir Richard Grenville, whose last battle in H.M.S. Revenge, off the Azores in 1591, and the part played in it by the 'Men of Bideford in Devon', was nobly lyricised by Lord Tennyson, the Poet Laureate from 1850 until 1892.

Derivation of Badge:
The badge is derived from the Seal of the town recorded in 1577, as is the present Arms of the Borough, granted to the town in 1936.

Badge Heritage:
1. A 'Shoreham' Class Escort Sloop, built by H.M. Dockyard, Devonport, launched in 1931 and sold for scrapping in 1949.

Notes:
The motto nearly yields the name of the ship.

The building of this ship by the premier warship building yard in Devonshire, was very appropriate.

MOD(N)

1931

Blazon: Per fess red and black;
    A gridiron gold.

Motto: Not recorded.

Date: 30.6.1949   **Frame:** Standard

Herald: Sir A. Cochrane

Derivation of Name:
Bigbury Bay is a stretch of coastal water between Stoke Point and Bolt Tail to the east of Plymouth, South Devonshire. The village of Bigbury, lying just inland, gives its name to the bay and Bigbury-on-Sea is a popular bathing spot. The name was selected in 1943 for one of a class of Frigates that were all named after bays in the United Kingdom.

Derivation of Badge:
The church in the village of Bigbury is a very prominent local feature, with its spire visible from any part of the bay. The patron Saint of this church is St. Lawrence, who, because of his beliefs during his service as Deacon of Pope Sixtus II, (circa 248 A.D.), was reputedly martyred by being roasted alive. The badge illustrates this legend, with its field colour of red – used in church decoration to symbolize martyrdom, and black – frequently used in Heraldry to denote grief and death. The gridiron, coloured gold to alude to glory, denotes the reputed instrument of the martyrdom of St. Lawrence.

Badge Heritage:
1. A 'Bay' Class Frigate, built by Hall Russell, launched in 1944 and sold in 1959 to the Portuguese Navy as the *Pacheco Pereira*.

Notes:
In common with the 'Castle' Class Corvettes, 'Bay' Class Frigates were not granted badges until after the War, due to the numbers involved.

During our research, we discovered that a representative from the College of Arms had visited Bigbury in 1949 to ascertain a suitable design for this badge. In the course of his research, he visited two ladies named Hooppell, whose family had lived in Bigbury for generations, and it is said that they would almost certainly have suggested that a reference to the village church should be included in the badge design.

Blazon: White; Issuant from a mural crown gold, a dexter arm embowed the hand grasping an inverted hammer disposed bendwise all proper.

Motto: Forward.

Date: 27.9.1921   **Frame:** Pentagon

Herald: C. ffoulkes

Derivation of Name:
Birmingham, the largest City in Warwickshire, is the commercial centre of the Midlands. The city has a very long history, one noteworthy occurrence being its sacking by Prince Rupert, during the English Civil War, in 1643. Since the Industrial Revolution, it has been a major industrial centre and was the birth-place of the brass trade.

Derivation of Badge:
This design was taken from the Crest of the Arms of the City of Birmingham, granted to them in 1889.

Their adoption of the Crest illustrates the industrial activity of the city, and in the badge it has been placed on a white field, this colour being used to provide contrast for the design.

Badge Heritage:
1. A 'Town' Class Cruiser, built by Armstrong, launched in 1913 and sold for scrapping in 1931.
2. A 'Town' Class Cruiser, built by H.M. Dockyard, Devonport, launched in 1936 and sold for scrapping in 1960.
3. A Type 42 Destroyer, built by Cammell Laird and launched in 1973.

Notes:
The motto of the ship is also that of the City.

The unofficial badge worn before 1921 by the 'Town' Class Cruiser of 1913 closely resembled the official badge, but with a naval crown instead of a mural one and this badge can still be seen in the Newcastle Museum of Science and Engineering.

MPL Neg. No.1074   1925

W & L   November 1937

W & L   September 1979

Blazon: Blue; A shark naiant bendwise clenched in its teeth a trident all gold.

Motto: Not recorded.

Date: 7.7.1943　　**Frame:** Standard

Herald: Sir A. Cochrane

Derivation of Name:
This name means one who, or that which, bites! This very aggressive name was originally a 'small ship' name* and was selected, in 1940, for one of a class of Escort Carriers, all of whose names ended in 'er'.

Derivation of Badge:
This design has used a shark to depict a 'biter', as this creature is well known as a 'biter' of the sea. Firmly held in its mouth is a trident, commonly used to depict naval weaponry, in this instance the aircraft embarked on board the ship.

Badge Heritage:
1. An 'Archer' Class Escort Carrier, built by Sun Shipbuilding, launched in 1940, and transferred under 'Lend-Lease' in 1941. Nominally returned to the United States, she was in fact transferred to the French Navy as the *Dixmude* in 1945.
2. An 'Archer' Class Coastal Training Craft, built by Watercraft Ltd. and completed in 1985.

Notes:
* During our research, we have found a note, (also confirmed by Manning and Walker's 'British Warship Names'), that these 'small ship' names were originally introduced into the Royal Navy in 1797, by the 2nd Earl of Spencer, George John, who served as First Lord of the Admiralty from 1794 to 1801 and derived from the names of the dogs in his foxhound pack.

This pack, the Pytchley hunt, still exists and research into this question is being undertaken by the Hon. Secretary of the hunt, Mr. D. Spilman.

MPL Neg. No.857　　　　　　　　　　　　　　　　　　1942

W. Sartori　　　　　　　　　　　　　　　　11th August 1986

Blazon: Green; A bittern alert proper.

Motto: Rostro Vindice. (Vengeance With My Beak.)

Date: 23.4.1934   **Frame:** Diamond

Herald: C. ffoulkes

Derivation of Name:
The bittern, *Botaurus stellaris*, is a genus of wading birds, belonging to the family *Ardeidae* and was once common to the British Isles. It is nocturnal, inhabiting swampy ground and is remarkable for its booming cry uttered during the breeding season. It needs to be approached with caution, as it will attack man or dog with its sharp beak and claws.

The name was chosen in 1933 for the first ship of the 'Bittern' Class Escort Sloops, all named after wading birds, but the first ship to be allocated this name was re-named H.M.S. Enchantress and completed as an Admiralty Yacht.

Derivation of Badge:
The badge has used the field colour, green, to denote the country habitat of this bird. A peculiarity of the bittern is the fact that it 'hides', with beak pointing skywards, whilst standing on one leg and from this position it is not easily roused. This stance has been depicted in the badge, with the bird shown in its proper colours. The very prominently-drawn beak and its position, may also have been used to allude to the very powerful anti-aircraft capability of the ship. 'See Motto.)

Badge Heritage:
1. A 'Bittern' Class Escort Sloop, built by White, launched in 1937 and sunk by German aircraft in Namsos Fiord on the 1st of May 1940, after being struck by a bomb on her quarterdeck, which set off her depth-charges, causing an uncontrollable fire. Miraculously, only eight of her crew were wounded and there was no loss of life.

Notes:
The motto as first submitted for approval was 'Rostro Vinco' — I Conquer With My Beak.

The unofficial badge for the Destroyer of 1897 also used a bittern as her badge, but depicted in a different attitude.

Blazon: Blue: A blackcap volant proper.

Motto: Not recorded.

Date: 18.12.1947   **Frame:** Standard

Herald: Sir A. Cochrane.

Derivation of Name:
The blackcap, *Sylvia atricapilla,* is a genus of song-birds belonging to the warbler group. Only the male bird has the distinctive jet-black cap which gives the name, as the hen's head feathers are brown. This name was selected in 1941 for a Fleet Air Arm Station and with very few exceptions, all R.N. airfields were, (and still are), named after various birds.

Derivation of Badge:
This badge shows a blackcap bird in flight, depicted in its proper colours, to illustrate the name and needs no further explanation.

Badge Heritage:
1. A Royal Naval Air Station at Stretton, Cheshire from 1942 until 1958.

Notes:
Post-war, this airfield was home to 1831 and 1841 Squadron of the Royal Naval Volunteer Reserve.

FAA Museum

Blazon: Per fess wavy red and blue;
A five-bar gate white.

Motto: Not recorded.

Date: 12.12.1941   **Frame:** Standard

Herald: Sir A. Cochrane

Derivation of Name:
Blackmore, or more correctly the 'Blackmore Vale', is a foxhound hunt that has taken its name from a fertile stretch of country on the border between Somerset and Dorset, running south from Wincanton, called the Vale of Blackmore. The hunt, with kennels at Sherborne, has been in existence since 1831, when the Rev. Harry Farr Yeatman hunted the area for fox, hare and roe deer. Since 1971 this foxhound hunt has been known as the Blackmore and Sparkford Vale'*. This name was selected in 1939 for one of the 'Hunt' Class Escort Destroyers ordered in that year.

Derivation of Badge:
The field colours of this badge match the colours of the hunt uniform, a red coat over a blue waistcoat, using a wavy division line in reference to the passage of the River Yeo, through the hunt country. The white five-bar gate has been taken from the Arms of the Yeatman family to recall the Rev. H. Yeatman's association with the hunt.

Badge Heritage:
1. A 'Hunt' Class Type II Escort Vessel, built by Stephen's, launched in 1941 and transferred to the Royal Danish Navy in 1952 as the *Esurn Snare*.

Notes:
* Throughout this work, information on the hunts will be given as it would have been available to the designer in the early 1940s, but any hunts that have subsequently changed their name will be noted.

The present hunt still retains the uniform of its predecessor.

G. Read Collection

15th January 1945

Blazon: Green: A roundel barry wavy of six white, and black, charged with a gull volant proper.

Motto: Not recorded.

Date: 10.9.1940   **Frame:** Standard

Herald: Sir A. Cochrane.

Derivation of Name:
Blackpool is a coastal town and well-known holiday resort in the county of Lancashire. The town owes its name to a large peaty-coloured pool or creek, now filled in, that formerly lay on the southern side of the present town. Through this creek, Marton Mere drained its peat discoloured water to the sea. The name was selected in 1938 for one of a class of Fleet Minesweepers that were all named after coastal towns of the United Kingdom; again in 1953 for one of a class of Frigates, whose names were taken from the same source.

Derivation of Badge:
The green field of the badge is in reference to the Fylde, a low lying peninsula, upon which Blackpool was built. The remainder of the design is derived from the Arms used by the Borough of Blackpool, that were granted to the town in 1899. The field of these Arms is gold and black, modified in the badge to white and black and presented in the form of a roundel, thus forming literally a 'black-pool'. The seagull is identical in both the Arms and the badge.

Badge Heritage:
1. A 'Bangor' Class Fleet Minesweeper, built by Harland & Wolff, launched in 1940 and sold for scrapping in 1946.
2. A 'Whitby' Class Frigate, built by Thornycroft, launched in 1957 and sold for scrapping in 1978. She was on loan to the Royal New Zealand Navy from 1966 until 1971.

Notes:
In the Arms of the town, the use of barry wavy gold and black indicated 'golden sand and black water'; the sand of the famous beach (The Golden Mile) and its 'black' water.

MOD(N)   June 1942

W & L   May 1965

Blazon: Blue; The head of the effigy of the Black Prince affrontee mailed and helmeted all white, crowned with a ducal coronet composed of seven strawberry leaves all gold, gemmed alternately red, and blue.

Motto: With High Courage.

Date: 6.11.1943   **Frame:** Standard

Herald: Sir A. Cochrane

Derivation of Name:
This name commemorates Edward, Prince of Wales, the eldest son of King Edward III.

Born in 1330, he was created Earl of Chester and Duke of Cornwall in 1337 and Prince of Wales in 1343. His military career began with the French campaign of 1346, where he distinguished himself both at Cressy and the Siege of Calais. He was one of the original Knights of the Garter and was present at the naval battle of Winchelsea against the Spaniards in 1349.*

Following his victory at the battle of Poictiers in 1356, he was created Duke of Aquitaine in 1362. His last major battle was his victory in 1367, at the Battle of Najera in Spain. He was obliged to return to England afterwards due to ill-health and this illness eventually forced him to resign his office of the Dukedom of Aquitaine in 1372. He died four years later and was buried in Canterbury Cathedral. Above the altar-tomb upon which his effigy lies, may still be seen some of his armour, his shield with its fleur-de-lys and lions, his surcoat, now faded to a dusty brown, his helmet and his gauntlets. His name of Black Prince was more likely due to the name he was called by the French, 'Le Noir' (the Black), on account of the gloom that his warlike deeds threw over their country, rather than the colour of his shield and armour, as the use of black armour was widespread in the 14th Century.

Derivation of Badge:
The head of the Black Prince in this badge design is an accurate depiction of his effigy in Canterbury Cathedral. It is coloured white, presumably in allusion to the fact that the design is derived from a statue**, whilst the coronet is shown proper to emphasise that the figure is that of a Prince.

Badge Heritage:
1. A Modified 'Dido' Class Light Cruiser, built by Harland & Wolff, launched in 1942 and transferred to the Royal New Zealand Navy in 1948. She was sold for scrapping in 1962.

Notes:
* This battle is supposed to be the first use of cannon by the English at sea.

** Research appears to indicate that where the design is derived from a statue, it is coloured white. If the statue is that of a king or queen, it is usually coloured gold, to denote royalty.

W & L

Blazon: White: Two barrulets wavy in base blue, the upper surmounted by a black swan statant proper.

Motto: Not recorded.

Date: 13.5.1938   **Frame:** Diamond

Herald: Sir A. Cochrane.

Derivation of Name:
The black swan, *Chenopis atrata,* is a rare species of this bird and is native only to Western Australia* and Tasmania. It was first discovered in 1697 by the Dutch explorer, Wilhelm de Vlaming, at what is now known as the Swan River, in Western Australia, the black swan's most important breeding ground. This name was selected in 1937 for the first ship of a class of sloops named after birds.

Derivation of Badge:
This design shows a black swan, in its proper colours, to give a simple illustration of the name.

Badge Heritage:
1. A 'Black Swan' Class Escort Sloop, built by Yarrow, launched in 1939, and sold for scrapping in 1956.

Notes:
* A black swan has been included in the Arms and Flag of Western Australia and also the State Arms of Australia.

A. J. Wilkinson   June 1950

Blazon: White; A roundel barry wavy of six white, and black, surmounted by a seax gold.

Motto: Not recorded.

Date: 3.7.1984   **Frame:** Standard

Herald: Sir W. Verco

Derivation of Name:
There are no fewer than thirteen rivers of this name in the United Kingdom, but the one honoured by this name is in Essex. It rises near Saffron Walden, in the north west of the county. In its upper reaches, above Braintree, it is called the River Pant. At Maldon, it widens into an estuary and enters the North Sea south of Brightlingsea. Sailing barges, once common in the estuary of this river, are still to be seen here during the annual barge races.

Derivation of Badge:
The wavy black and white roundel is used to denote 'black' water to give a pun on the name of the river. The gold seax has also been used as a pun, in this instance on the name of the County where the river is located, thus avoiding confusion with any of the other twelve rivers of this name. Both the Counties of Essex and Middlesex use this device in their Arms but coloured silver with a golden pommel and hilt.

Badge Heritage:
1. A 'River' Class Minesweeper, built by Richards and launched in 1984.

Notes:
Nearly all of the 'River' Class Minesweepers are manned by the Royal Naval Reserve, but H.M.S. Backwater is currently (1988) manned by the Royal Navy and used on Fishery Protection duties.

Navpic

10th December 1985

Blazon: Blue: Surmounting two barrulets wavy in base white, an oar bendwise proper, surmounted by a crescent silver, between the horns a mascle white.

Motto: Straightforward.

Date: 28.4.1955   **Frame:** Standard

Herald: M. R. Trappes-Lomax

Derivation of Name:
This name commemorates Sir Henry Blackwood (1770-1832), Vice-Admiral of the Blue, 1st Baron Blackwood and Lord Dufferin and Clanboye. Entering the Royal Navy at eleven years of age, he was in action at "The Glorious First of June", 1794, and when in command of H.M.S. Penelope in March 1800, won great credit in his fight with the French ship-of-the-Line, *Guillaume Tell*. He was one of Lord Nelson's favourite Frigate Captains and commanded H.M.S. Euryalus at the Battle of Trafalgar.

Captain Blackwood remained on active service until 1815 and served in the Royal Navy until 1830. He was created Baron Blackwood in 1815 and died on the 17th of December 1832.

This name was first selected in 1942 for one of a class of 'Lend-Lease' Destroyer-Escorts classified as Frigates in the Royal Navy, all named after successful Royal Naval Frigate Captains.*

Derivation of Badge:
The crescent and the mascle are from the Arms of Sir Henry Blackwood, namely: 'blue; a fess gold, in chief a crescent silver, between two mullets gold, and in base a mascle silver'. From these Arms, the field colour is also derived, whilst the oar records an incident that occurred whilst he was in command of H.M.S. Ajax (the second of the name – a 3rd Rate), during an expedition to force the Dardanelles, under the command of Vice-Admiral John Duckworth. Capt. Blackwood had a narrow escape from death when his ship accidentally caught fire on the 11th of February 1807, off the island of Tenedos and sank with the loss of two hundred and fifty of her crew. He survived by clinging to an oar until he was rescued by H.M.S. Canopus.

Badge Heritage:
1. A 'Blackwood' Class Frigate, built by Thornycroft, launched in 1955 and sold for scrapping in 1976.

Notes:
* Neither the first ship of this name, nor any of her sisters, were granted badges, due to the exigencies of the War.

The first ship to wear this badge was one of a class of Frigates named after Nelson's Frigate Captains.

Blazon: Blue; A martlet white, within a circle of chain the ends conjoined and extended in base gold.

Motto: More Majorem. (After The Manner Of Our Ancestors.)

Date: 16.5.1946   **Frame:** Standard

Herald: Sir A. Cochrane

Derivation of Name:
This name commemorates Robert Blake (1599-1657). Little is known of his early life, but he rose to prominence during the English Civil War. He was appointed General of the Fleet by Cromwell in 1649 and sent to fight the Royalist Fleet under the command of Prince Rupert. Blake destroyed this fleet in 1650 off the coast of Spain, an action which induced the Spanish government to recognise the Commonwealth. On the 4th of September 1652, he destroyed a French squadron which was on its way to relieve Dunkirk, thus making it necessary for the town to surrender and forcing France to copy the example of Spain. England declared war on the Dutch in 1652 and the struggle resolved itself into a series of naval engagements in which Blake was the leading figure. He is best known for his resounding victory on the 18th-20th of February 1653 off Portland, when, whilst flying his flag in H.M.S. Triumph, he defeated Tromp's Dutch fleet.

Derivation of Badge:
The white martlet is derived from the Crest of the Arms of Admiral Blake. The chain denotes the fact that, for his distinguished services during the Dutch War, Admiral Blake was presented by Parliament in 1658 with a Dutch War Medal in gold* and a gold chain worth £300 at the time.

Badge Heritage:
1. A 'Minotaur' Class Cruiser**, built by Fairfield and launched in 1945. Building was suspended from 1946 until 1954 but she was completed in 1961. Later converted to a Helicopter Command Cruiser during 1965-1969, she was sold for scrapping in 1982.

Notes:
* Only four of these large oval medals were granted in gold.
  **This ship was laid down and launched as a unit of the 'Minotaur' Class. In 1954 she was reclassified as one of the 'Tiger' Class and was the last cruiser to serve in the Royal Navy.

MPL Neg. No.1469

July 1960

Blazon: White: A lion rampant grasping in its forepaws a sword its point enfiled by a wreath of laurel all proper.

Motto: Dum Spiro Spero. (Whilst I Breathe I Hope)

Date: 11.9.1929   **Frame:** Shield

Herald: C. ffoulkes

Derivation of Name:
This is a prize name, formerly the French *Blanche*, captured on the 21st of December 1779 by H.M.S. Suffolk and H.M.S. Magnificent off St. Lucia.

Derivation of Badge:
This design perpetuates the memory of the tenth ship of the name. A Light Cruiser, she was present at the Battle of Jutland on the 31st of May 1916, under the command of Captain J. M. Casement R.N. Her role was to repeat signals between units of the Grand Fleet and this vital task was well executed, Captain Casement being mentioned in the despatches of Admiral Sir John Jellicoe. He later rose to Flag rank, retiring with the rank of Admiral. The complete design is part of his Arms. The use of white as the field colour in the design alludes to the name itself and also to its origin. The French word *'blanche'* is the feminine of *'blanc'* — both words meaning 'white'.

Badge Heritage:
1. A 'B' Class Destroyer built by Hawthorn-Leslie, launched in 1930 and lost on the 13th of November 1939 in the Thames Estuary after striking a mine.

Notes:
The motto of the ship is also that of Admiral Casement.

W & L   August 1936

Blazon: Red; Two hunting horns in saltire white, surmounted by a griffin's head erazed gold.

Motto: Not recorded.

Date: 25.3.1942   **Frame:** Standard

Herald: Sir A. Cochrane

Derivation of Name:
Blankney is the name of a foxhound hunt which covers an area on the borders of Lincolnshire and Nottinghamshire, taking its title from a village to the south of Lincoln. Although the hunt dates from 1871, it was reconstituted in 1895 in its present form.

The name was selected in 1941 for a 'Hunt' Class Escort Vessel.

Derivation of Badge:
The red field of the badge denotes the colour of the coats worn by the hunt, whilst the two hunting horns are symbols linking the sport of hunting with the class of ship. The gold griffin's head has been adapted from the Arms of the Chaplin family to recall that it was this family that provided the Mastership of the hunt between 1871 and 1885.

Badge Heritage:
1. A 'Hunt' Class Type II Escort Vessel, built by J. Brown, launched in 1940 and sold for scrapping in 1959.

Notes:
On the return of this ship from abroad to the U.K. in 1945, she was placed in reserve at Devonport and saw no further service.

MOD(N)

June 1943

Blazon: Blue: A star of six points the lower point extended and the points interspaced with rays all gold, between two lesser stars fesswise in perspective also of six points silver.

Motto: Not recorded.

Date: 2.7.1985   **Frame:** Standard

Herald: Sir W. Verco

Derivation of Name:
It is thought that the original intention of the meaning of this name was to denote one who 'blazes' a trail, by marking a path for others to follow.*

Derivation of Badge:
The badge design illustrates an alternative meaning of the name as it shows a 'super nova', placed in front of two smaller stars, all on a blue field depicting the night sky; in effect, a celestial 'blazer'.

Badge Heritage:
1. An 'Archer' Class Coastal Training Craft laid down in 1985 by Watercraft Marine and not yet completed.

Notes:
* This name was introduced into the Royal Navy by Earl Spencer in 1797 and for an explanation of this, please see the notes for H.M.S. Biter.

Navpic

August 1986

Blazon: Green; A hunting horn white, and a battle-axe gold, in saltire.

Motto: Not recorded.

Date: 28.4.1942   **Frame:** Standard

Herald: Sir A. Cochrane

Derivation of Name:
Blean is the name of a foot beagle hunt with its kennels at Hernhill, near Faversham, Kent. The name is adopted from that of a medieval forest which covered the coastline of Kent between Rochester and Dover. The hunt was founded in 1909 by Mr William Charles Dawes*, then Master of the Tickham fox-hounds. The name was introduced into the Royal Navy in 1941 for one of the 'Hunt' Class Escort Vessels.

Derivation of Badge:
The walking huntsmen wear the traditional coat of 'Beagle green' and this colour is reflected in the field colour of the badge. A white hunting horn is included in the design to denote the sport of hunting and also possibly as a link between the sport and the class of ship for which the badge was designed. The golden battleaxe is derived from the crest of the Dawes family and commemorates this family's connection with the hunt.

Badge Heritage:
1. A 'Hunt' Class Type III Escort Vessel, built by Hawthorn-Leslie, launched in 1942 and lost on the 11th of December 1942 after being torpedoed by *U-443*, west of Oran, with the loss of 89 ratings.

Notes:
* Mr William Dawes, after establishing the Blean hunt in 1909, presented its Mastership to his then eight-year old daughter. Today, almost eighty years later, his daughter, now Mrs J. B. McKeever, still holds that post.

    The writers wish to thank Mrs J. B. McKeever for her valuable assistance in researching this and other sporting hunts.

Blazon: Blue: Two hunting horns in saltire white, surmounted by a hare courant gold.

Motto: Not recorded.

Date: 21.1.1942   **Frame:** Standard

Herald: Sir A. Cochrane

Derivation of Name:
Bleasdale, a small village to the south-east of Lancaster, is the name adopted by a foot Beagle hunt, previously known as the 'Oakenclough Beagles'. The kennels are at Longridge and the hunt country covers part of the shore-line of Lancashire and Cumberland, including fells up to 2,000 feet high.

Derivation of Badge:
This badge design shows a pair of hunting horns to denote the sport of hunting and a hare at speed denoting the hunt quarry.

Badge Heritage:
1. A 'Hunt' Class Type III Escort Vessel, built by Vickers-Armstrong, launched in 1941 and sold for scrapping in 1956.

Notes:
The uniform of this hunt is 'Beagle green' with a red collar, but for reasons unknown, these colours were not included in the badge.

In June 1947, this ship was reclassified as an Anti-Aircraft Frigate.

Blazon: Red; A crozier and a hunting horn in saltire all gold.

Motto: Not recorded.

Date: 3.4.1942*   **Frame:** Standard

Herald: Sir A. Cochrane

Derivation of Name:
Blencathra is the name of a foxhunt in Cumberland that takes its title from a 2,800 ft. summit to the north of Keswick. Locally, this hunt is often referred to as the 'John Peel Foxhounds', as many of the present hounds' pedigrees can be traced back to the 'Peel' pack.

The hunt country, being nearly all mountainous, can only be hunted on foot.

Derivation of Badge:
The field colour, red, denotes the hunt uniform and a hunting horn is included in the design to denote the sport of hunting. The hunt Master was Mr John Crozier from 1839, until his death in 1903. He was not entitled to armorial bearings, so an ecclesiastical crozier has been used as a 'cant', (or pun), upon his name, to commemorate his long term of office with the hunt.

Badge Heritage:
1. A 'Hunt' Class Type I Escort Vessel, built by Cammell-Laird, launched in 1940 and sold for scrapping in 1957.

Notes:
* This ship was completed in December 1940, and commissioned shortly afterwards, but the writers have found no explanation of the late grant of a badge. Comparison of completion dates of the 'Hunt' class with the dates of approval of their badges reveal that this is the only instance where this delay occurred.

It has been noticed during our researches that a number of incorrect explanations of badges are on file in MOD(N) records. The crozier in the design of this badge is given as referring to a Mr Bishop, a Master of the hunt, but Mr M. J. Thompson, the present Honorary Secretary of the Blencathra hunt, has confirmed that the name of Bishop does not appear in their very complete record of hunt Masters.

G. Read Collection   February 1944

Blazon: Black: A lion rampant silver.

Motto: Amat Victoria Curam. (Victory And Prudence Are Friends.)

Date: 29.7.1921   **Frame:** Diamond

Herald: C. ffoulkes

Derivation of Name:
This name commemorates the Battle of Blenheim, fought on the 13th of August 1704. This great battle was fought midway between Blindheim (of which Blenheim is a corruption) and Hochstadt in Bavaria, where the allied armies, under the command of the Duke of Marlborough and Prince Eugene of Savoy, defeated the French and Bavarians under Marshal Tallard, Marshal Marsin and the Elector of Bavaria during the war of the Spanish Succession. The Duke of Marlborough's brilliant strategy ensured a decisive victory and freed Austria from the menace of invasion during the campaign. A grateful Parliament presented the Duke of Marlborough with a large country manor near Woodstock, Oxfordshire, and it was named Blenheim Park.* Several senior officers received decorations, nor were the rank and file forgotten, every man present at the battle received a month's wages as a bonus, and every man wounded received three month's extra wages.

Derivation of Badge:
This design is from the Arms of John Churchill, 1st Duke of Marlborough, granted to him on the 14th of December 1702. These Arms include a silver lion on a black field.**

Badge Heritage:
1. A 1st Class Cruiser built by Thames Ironworks, launched in 1890, converted to a Depot Ship in 1907 and sold for scrapping in 1926.
2. A Depot Ship purchased in 1940 (ex. *S.S. Achilles*) and sold for scrapping in 1948.

Notes:
The motto refers to the campaigns of the Duke of Marlborough.

 * Blenheim is still the seat of the current Duke of Marlborough and the trees in the grounds of this very beautiful mansion were reputed to have been planted to denote the positions of Marlborough's troops during the battle.

 ** The life of the 1st Duke and his descendants have inspired five ship's badges and the naming of no less than twenty-three Royal Naval warships.

G. Read Collection

W & L   February 1946

Blazon: White; A bell blue, banded and clappered gold.

Motto: Ring True.

Date: 29.7.1921   **Frame:** Diamond

Herald: C. ffoulkes

Derivation of Name:
The Bluebell, *Scilla non-scripta*, is a species of wild flower very common in woodlands of the United Kingdom. The name is derived from the colour and the shape of its petals which are clustered together in the form of a bell.

This name was selected in 1914 for one of a class of Sloops all named after flowers.

Derivation of Badge:
The design illustrates another version of a 'blue bell', in this instance a church bell, coloured blue to denote fidelity* and decorated gold. The design has been placed on a white field and the use of this colour is to denote purity.**

Badge Heritage:
1. A 'Flower' Class (Acacia Group) Sloop built by Scott, launched in 1915 and sold for scrapping in 1931.

Notes:
It is not thought that the 'Flower' Class Corvette of this name, built by Fleming and Ferguson and launched in 1940, wore this badge because, as previously noted, the Ship's Badges Committee decided that Corvettes were not to be granted badges during hostilities due to the sheer numbers involved.

The motto alludes to the 'true*' (clear, pure**) sound of a well constructed bell.

G. Read Collection   27th June 1920

Blazon: Blue: A demi-lion erazed gold, langued red, grasping in its forepaws a coal-pick black.

Motto: Not recorded.

Date: 21.8.1940   **Frame:** Diamond

Herald: Sir A. Cochrane

Derivation of Name:
Blyth is a seaport in the County of Northumberland, nine miles east-south-east of Morpeth and is situated at the mouth of the river of the same name. The town's chief industry is the export of the coal mined in the district, but several ship-building yards are also located in the town.

The name was selected in 1939 for one of a class of Fleet Minesweepers named after seaside towns in the United Kingdom.

Derivation of Badge:
This design is adapted from the Crest to the Arms of the Borough of Blyth, granted to them on the 24th of January 1924. This crest shows a golden lion grasping in its paws a miner's lamp, rising from a mural crown which has three miners' picks placed upon it. The designer has removed the lamp from the paws of the lion and replaced it with a coal-pick; the badge therefore, gives a direct reference to the origin of the name.

Badge Heritage:
1. A 'Bangor' Class Fleet Minesweeper built by Blyth Shipbuilders, launched in 1940 and sold for civilian use in 1948.

Notes:
The ties between the town and the ship were very strong during World War II, a very happy association being formed from the moment her keel was laid.

W & L

February 1946

Blazon: Black; The erect figure of Queen Boadicea with arms upraised in her dexter hand a spear and flanked by her kneeling daughters all mounted upon a scythed chariot drawn by two horses forcene all gold.

Motto: Vincta Sed Invicta. (Bound (lashed) But Unconquered.)

Date: 15.8.1929   **Frame:** Shield

Herald: D.N.E.*

Derivation of Name:
The history of Boadicea, Queen of the Iceni, did not come to light until the early 16th Century, when the works of the Roman historian Tacitus were discovered and published in Italy. The name is mistranslated from Boudicca, a name of Gaelic origin meaning 'Victoria'. Her husband, King Prasutagus, a tenant king in what is now the County of Norfolk, died in 59 A.D., and he stipulated in his Will that his kingdom was to be divided between the Emperor Nero and his two daughters. But, in collecting the Emperor's legacy, the Procurator confiscated the entire kingdom, dispossessed the Icenian nobles and carried off the ablebodied as slaves. The worst outrage occurred at the royal palace when Prasutagus' two daughters were raped and Boudicca stripped and flogged. The remnants of the Iceni under her leadership together with the Trinovantes, a neighbouring tribe, took up arms against the Romans and a short but bloody campaign began. The important Roman garrison towns of *Camulodunum* (Colchester), *Verulamium* (St. Albans), and *Londinium* (London) were laid waste and the elite Ninth Legion were slaughtered to a man, probably near Cambridge, before Boudicca's force was defeated in battle by seasoned Roman troops near Atherstone in 60 A.D. Boudicca escaped the final massacre and is presumed to have committed suicide rather than fall into the hands of the Romans.

Derivation of Badge:
The design closely follows that of an earlier unofficial badge for the third ship of the name, both inspired by the large bronze statue of Boadicea facing the House of Commons from the northwest corner of Westminster Bridge, sculptured by Thomas Thorneycroft and erected in 1902. The field colour, black, is used to signify the mourning and death of Boadicea, whilst the gold of the design indicates her royal status.

Badge Heritage:
1. A 'B' Class Destroyer built by Hawthorn-Leslie, launched in 1930 and lost on the 13th of June 1944, whilst under the command of Lieut.-Cdr. F. W. Hawkins R.N., with the loss of nine officers and 166 ratings off Portland after being torpedoed by German aircraft. Cdr. Hawkins was one of the officers killed.

Notes:
* The sealed pattern for this badge consists only of its surround, a note within stating that this design was suggested by the D.N.E., (Rear-Admiral J. W. Henley, Chairman, S.B.C.) and attached, a photo of a tampion from the previous ship. From this it was left to the wood-carver's skill to produce an attractive badge. The coloured illustration of this badge was drawn by Mr. Clive Birchall, DML Ltd., from the carving held in the Pattern Shop at Devonport Dockyard. Post-war, it was intended to give this name to the WRNS Depot at Burghfield, but it was jocularly pointed out that certain Wrens were war-like enough already, without giving them further encouragement!

Blazon: Barry wavy of six white and blue;
A wyvern with wings extended all red, statant within a horseshoe inverted gold, all inclined to profile.

Motto: Not recorded.

Date: 11.6.1940   **Frame:** Pentagon

Herald: Sir A. Cochrane

Derivation of Name:
The word 'bonaventure' is thought to have been derived from the Italian word 'bonaventura', which translates literally as 'good venture' and over the years has come to be expressive of good luck.

Derivation of Badge:
A horseshoe has long been used to symbolise good luck and is used in this design for the same purpose. The red wyvern is taken from the Arms claimed by Sir Francis Drake and commemorates his voyage to the West Indies whilst commanding the third ship of the name*. (Drake sailed from Plymouth in March 1585, plundered Vigo, captured San Domingo, pillaged Carthagena, San Antonio, Santa Elena and San Augustine and captured many Spanish treasure-ships before returning to Portsmouth in July 1586.) In this ship he also fought the famous action at Cadiz in 1587, an occasion passed down in history in which he was said to have 'singed the beard of the King of Spain'.

Badge Heritage:
1. A 'Dido' Class Light Cruiser built by Scotts, launched in 1939 and lost on the 31st March 1941, whilst under the command of Capt. H. J. Egerton R.N., with the loss of twenty-three officers and one hundred and sixteen ratings after being torpedoed by the Italian Submarine *Ambra* south of Crete.
2. A Submarine Depot Ship built by Greenock Dockyard, launched in 1942 and sold for scrapping in 1948.

Notes:
The Light Fleet Carrier H.M.S. Powerful was sold to the Royal Canadian Navy in 1956 and renamed *H.M.C.S. Bonaventure*.

Title to this name then passed to Canada and the badge was transferred at the same time. The design remained virtually the same with the addition of a collar of maple leaves around the neck of the wyvern.

* His flagship was actually named the Elizabeth Bonaventure.

Husbands of Bristol   1939

W & L   May 1947

Blazon: Blue; A stag's head caboshed gold, between its attires a plate charged with a fleur-de-lys blue.

Motto: Not recorded.

Date: 3.4.1942   **Frame:** Standard

Herald: Sir A. Cochrane

Derivation of Name:

Bootle is a Lancashire seaport comprising the townships of Bootle-cum-Linacre and Orrel. The docks, which are some of the finest on the River Mersey, belong to the port of Liverpool.*

The name was first selected in 1918 for one of a class of Minesweepers all named after towns of the United Kingdom and again in 1940 for one of a class of Fleet Minesweepers all named after coastal towns of the United Kingdom.

Derivation of Badge:

The design is derived from the Arms of the County Borough of Bootle, granted on the 4th of November 1869. These Arms, (which were partially derived from the Earl of Derby's), show three gold stag's heads on a blue chevron and three blue fleur-de-lys on a white field. The badge thus gives a direct reference to the town honoured by the name of the ship.

Badge Heritage:

1. A 'Bangor' Class Fleet Minesweeper built by Ailsa Shipbuilders, launched in 1941 and sold for scrapping in 1948.

Notes:
* The reader should bear in mind that facts relating to the badge designs are presented as they would have been when the badge was designed.

IWM Neg. No.FL2707

circa 1943

Blazon: Black; Issuant bendwise from sinister the winged demi-figure of Boreas gold, issuing from his mouth a representation of the wind silver.

Motto: Vente Favente. (With Favouring Wind.)

Date: 4.7.1929   **Frame:** Shield

Herald: C. ffoulkes

Derivation of Name:
Boreas, in Greek Mythology, was the personification of the North wind, a son of the Titan Astraeus and Eos (the stars and the dawn), and brother of Eurus, Zephyrus, and Notus. He dwelt in a cave on Mount Haemus in Thrace. He courted and forcibly carried off Orithyia, a daughter of Erechtheus, King of Attica. He sired three children, Zetes, Calais, and Cleopatra. According to legend, during the first Persian war, Boreas aided the Athenians by destroying the ships of the Persians by storms and he was afterwards worshipped at Athens, where a festival called Boreasmi was celebrated in his honour.

Derivation of Badge:
This badge shows Boreas creating a storm of the North wind. A storm from the north is usually cold and bitter, very destructive and accompanied by dark skies. The design intimates this both by the use of a black field and the placing of the stream of wind.

Badge Heritage:
1. A 'B' Class Destroyer built by Palmer, launched in 1930. She was lent to the Greek Navy from 1944 until 1951 serving as the *Salamis** and sold for scrapping in 1951.

Notes:
* By a curious coincidence, the name given to this ship by the Greeks during her service with them was the scene in 480 B.C. of the famous naval victory of the Greeks over the Persians. Boreas, helping to defeat the Persians in legend and Salamis, the scene of their defeat in fact.

The motto also refers to the wind.

W & L   July 1931

Blazon: Barry wavy of ten white and blue;
A falcon close proper, belled gold, its dexter talon supporting a rose red, barbed and seeded proper.

Motto: Not recorded.

Date: 8.1.1946   **Frame:** Standard

Herald: Sir A. Cochrane

Derivation of Name:
This name commemorates Admiral the Hon. Edward Boscawen (1711-1761). The second son of the 1st Viscount Falmouth, he entered the Royal Navy in 1726. Whilst in command of H.M.S. Namur, he took part in Lord Anson's victory over the French on the 3rd of May 1747, off Cape Finisterre.

In the same year he was made Commander-in-Chief of the East Indies, receiving the surrender of Madras. He was Commander-in-Chief at the fall of Louisburg, Cape Breton Island in 1758, and on the 17th of August 1759, he defeated the French fleet off Gibraltar, destroying its remnants in Lagos Bay the following day. In 1760 he was appointed General of Marines and he died on the 10th of January 1761.

Derivation of Badge:
This design is derived from the Arms and Crest of Admiral Edward Boscawen. These Arms include a red rose on a field of ermine. The falcon is reproduced in the badge design as it appears in the Crest, but with its talon supporting the rose.

Badge Heritage:
1. H.M. Naval Base Portland, Dorset, commissioned in 1932 and paid off in 1947.

Notes:
An aerial photograph of Portland taken between 1932 and 1947 was not obtainable. We have included therefore, an aerial photo taken in the late 1960s, courtesy of Mr Lovell of the Fleet Air Museum, Yeovilton.

FAA Museum

circa 1970

Blazon: Blue; A trident enfiled by three Royal coronets in pale all gold.

Motto: Not recorded.

Date: 7.7.1942   **Frame:** Standard

Herald: Sir A. Cochrane

Derivation of Name:
The first ship of this name (and the four that followed), were named after the town of Boston, Mass., U.S.A. This name was not then used for one hundred and thirty-nine years, but when it was resurrected in 1940 for one of a class of Minesweepers, all named after coastal towns of the United Kingdom, the derivation was from Boston*, Lincolnshire. The town has a corporation dock with an area of seven acres and deep sea fishing with a fleet of forty trawlers and has proved very prosperous. In Plantagenet times, Boston was a chief port of the kingdom and much frequented by traders of the Hanseatic League.

Derivation of Badge:
This design is partially derived from the Arms of the Borough of Boston as recorded during the Visitation of Heralds on the 1st of December 1568. These Arms include three Royal coronets, but for the badge the designer has placed them on a blue field enfiling a golden trident. A trident is often seen in Naval heraldry as a symbol of sea-power. The design links the town with the ship of the same name and also denotes the Royal Navy's mastery of the sea.

Badge Heritage:
1. A 'Bangor' Class Fleet Minesweeper built by Ailsa Shipbuilders, launched in 1940 and sold for scrapping in 1948.

Notes:
* The name 'Boston' is a corruption of 'Bottolphs's town' as St Botolph founded a monastery on the site of the present town in 654 A.D.

September 1943

Blazon: Red; A dexter boxing glove apaumee white, corded and edged gold.

Motto: Praemonitus Praemunitus. (Forewarned Is Forearmed.)*

Date: 3.7.1947   **Frame:** Standard

Herald: Sir A. Cochrane

Derivation of Name:

A boxer is one who participates in fist-fights to a set of rules and with gloves, (a pugilist.)

This is another name introduced by Earl Spencer in 1797 and, as mentioned earlier, is thought to be from the name of one of his foxhounds.

Derivation of Badge:

This design displays a white boxing glove on a red field. The field colour denotes combat and the glove, presented Heraldically, is white in order to avoid placing a coloured charge on a red field.

The badge is a simple illustration of the meaning of the name.

Badge Heritage:

1. A Radar Training Ship built by Harland & Wolff, launched in 1942 as a Tank Landing Ship**, converted to a Fighter Direction Ship in 1944 and converted again in 1947 as a Radar Training Ship. She was sold for scrapping in 1958.
2. A Type 22 Frigate built by Yarrow and launched in 1981.

Notes:

* This motto was used by the first ship to wear the badge and alluded to her role of radar training.

**During the Second World War, she took part in the invasion of Sicily and Italy.

W & L   September 1947

Navpic   17th October 1983

Blazon: Blue; A lion rampant between four billets one two and one all gold.

Motto: Je Maintiendrai. (I Will Maintain.)

Date: 23.4.1934   **Frame:** Diamond

Herald: C. ffoulkes

Derivation of Name:
This name originally commemorated the Battle of the Boyne, which took place three miles from Drogheda on the 30th of June 1690. This battle was fought between the forces of James II and King William III of Orange, James II being defeated and later taking exile in France. In 1903 the derivation was changed to denote the river of the same name, which rises near the village of Carberry, Co. Kildare, and enters the Irish Sea a little below Drogheda after a course of about seventy miles.

Derivation of Badge:
This design follows the original derivation of the name, but indicates the river, albeit obliquely, as the battle was fought on both of its banks. The badge is derived from the Arms of the victor of the battle, King William III of Orange.

Badge Heritage:
1. A 'River' Class Trawler built by Cochrane, launched in 1918, named in 1920 and sold for civilian use in 1946.

Notes:
The motto is also that of William III.

MPL Neg. No.3258

1936

Blazon: Blue; A ram's head erazed affrontee white, armed gold, gorged with a mural crown also gold, charged with a hurt, thereon a mullet white.

Motto: Not recorded.

Date: 18.11.1941   **Frame:** Standard

Herald: Sir A. Cochrane

Derivation of Name:
Bradford is a City in the West Riding of Yorkshire. From the Middle Ages, for three centuries or more, woollen manufacturing was its staple industry. The drift of the worsted trade from East Anglia to the North began in the 17th Century and since 1798, when the first worsted mill was erected in Bradford, the city has become the centre of the worsted, yarn and soft goods industry in Britain. It was here that Dr Edmund Cartwright (1743-1823) invented the power loom and it is also the home of the famous Black Dyke Mills brass band. This name was first introduced into the Royal Navy because of Bradford's Parliamentarian associations and was revived in 1940 for one of a class of destroyers said to be named after towns and cities common to both the United Kingdom and the United States. The other city this name commemorates is in McKean County, Pennsylvania and first settled in 1823. It was laid out as a town in 1838 and named Littleton, but the present name was substituted in 1858, in honour of William Bradford (1755-1795).

Derivation of Badge:
This design is inspired by the supporters to the Arms of the City of Bradford. These supporters are a black ram with gold horns and a white angora goat. The designer has combined some features of both, adding a mural crown around the neck to symbolise the City. The hurt with its mullet is a representation of the U.S. Military Forces emblem and denotes that this ship was one of the fifty destroyers transferred from the United States in 1940.

Badge Heritage:
1. A 'Town' Class Destroyer built by Bethlehem, launched in 1918 which served in the U.S. Navy as the *U.S.S. McLanahan*. She was named H.M.S. Bradford in 1940 and sold for scrapping in 1946.

Notes:
The ship's badge of this warship was one of those sent to the United States post-war as mentioned earlier in this volume. Is it still in City Hall, Bradford, McKean County?

Husbands of Bristol

1942

Blazon: White; A sprig of bramble slipped leaved blossomed and fructed all proper.

Motto: Not recorded.

Date: 13.5.1938   **Frame:** Diamond

Herald: Sir A. Cochrane

Derivation of Name:
The bramble, *Rubus fruticosus*, is a fruit-bearing shrub, (also called blackberry) and a member of the order *Rosaceae*. It is thought that this very old 'small-ship' name was introduced originally because of the numerous thorns found on the bush. (A thorn in the side of the enemy.)

Derivation of Badge:
This very attractive design yields a straightforward illustration of the name and needs no further explanation.

Badge Heritage:
1. A 'Halcyon' Class Fleet Minesweeper, built by H.M. Dockyard, Devonport and launched in 1938. She was sunk in the Barents Sea by gunfire from the German cruiser *Hipper* and two German destroyers on the 31st of December 1942, whilst under the command of Cdr. H. T. Rust D.S.O., R.N., with the loss of all of her ships' company, (eight officers and one hundred and thirteen ratings), whilst escorting Convoy JW51B* from Loch Ewe to Russia.
2. An 'Algerine' Class Fleet Minesweeper, built by Lobnitz, launched in 1945 and sold for scrapping in 1961.

Notes:
* This convoy was engaged by substantial German surface forces (*Lutzow, Hipper* and six destroyers) but due to the skill and bravery of the escort, all of the merchant ships reached their destination safely.

Husbands of Bristol   1941

W & L   June 1953

Blazon: Barry wavy of six white and blue;
A fox sejant red, its tail erect.

Motto: Not recorded.

Date: 12.12.1941   **Frame:** Standard

Herald: Sir A. Cochrane

Derivation of Name:
Bramham, or more correctly, 'Bramham Moor', is the name of a foxhound hunt covering part of the West Riding of Yorkshire, to the south-east of Wetherby. It takes its title from a moor of the same name* within the hunt country. Documents verify that this hunt was established in 1750 by Mr. James Fox-Lane, the nephew of Baron Bingley. The present family, whose name evolved to Lane-Fox, still maintain their early connection with the hunt.

Derivation of Badge:
The field of wavy white and blue bars denotes the River Wharfe, which flows through the hunt country.

The seated red fox is taken from the Crest of the Arms of the Fox-Lane family and is included in the design to recall the founder of the hunt. Conveniently, this charge can also refer to the colour of the hunt uniform coat and the quarry of the hounds.

Badge Heritage:
1. A 'Hunt' Class Type II Escort Vessel, built by Stephen's and launched in 1942. She was transferred on loan to the Greek Navy in 1943 and served as *Themistoklis* until 1959. She was sold for scrapping in 1960.

Notes:
* This moor, near Tadcaster, was the scene of the Battle of Bramham Moor, fought on the 29th of February 1408, during which Henry, 1st Earl of Northumberland, 4th Lord Percy of Alnwick, was killed.

MOD(N)   August 1942

Blazon: White; The war-bonnet of a North American Plains Indian proper.

Motto: Fortis Fortuna Adjuvat.* (Fortune Favours The Brave.)

Date: 21.5.1943   **Frame:** Standard

Herald: Sir A. Cochrane

Derivation of Name:
The adjective 'brave' means courageous, intrepid, stout-hearted or, as a verb, to meet or face danger with bravery; to encounter.

Derivation of Badge:
This design illustrates another meaning of the word 'brave', i.e. a warrior of the North American Indians. The intricate design shows a war-bonnet of an Oglala Sioux Indian brave, placed on a white field to provide contrast.

Badge Heritage:
1. An 'Algerine' Class Fleet Minesweeper built by Blyth Shipbuilders, launched in 1943 and renamed H.M.S. Satellite in 1951 for her new role as an R.N.V.R. Drillship. She was sold for scrapping in 1958.
2. A Type 22 Frigate built by Yarrow and launched in 1983.

Notes:
The Sioux, more than any other Plains Indian tribe, developed a 'feather heraldry', by which eagle feathers, beads and other devices worn in the hair or in the head-dress, told of the wearer's achievements.

    * This motto was chosen by the ship's company of the second ship to wear the badge.

MPL Neg. No.2636   March 1944

Navpic   9th June 1986

H.M.S. BRAZEN (1781)

Blazon: Red; A Roman Cornua viroled all gold.

Motto: Audax Omnia Perpeti. (Bold To Endure All Things.)

Date: 4.7.1929 **Frame:** Shield

Herald: C. ffoulkes

Derivation of Name:
The verb 'brazen' means 'to make bold', or 'to face impudently', most suitable for a 'small-ship' name! As an adjective it means 'made of brass'.

Derivation of Badge:
The alternative meaning of the name was chosen to inspire the design of this badge. The term 'brazen trumpets' is well known, and because a Latin motto was to be given to the ship, a Latin trumpet (the Roman cornua) would be very appropriate. It has been placed on a red field to symbolise martialism.

Badge Heritage:
1. A 'B' Class Destroyer built by Palmer, launched in 1930 and sunk by German aircraft off Dover on the 20th of July 1940, whilst under the command of Lieut.-Cdr. Sir Michael Culme-Seymour R.N., one rating died of wounds.
2. A Type 22 Frigate built by Yarrow and launched in 1980.

Notes:
The motto alludes to the meaning of the word 'brazen' when used as a verb.

W & L   February 1931

Navpic   21st June 1984

Blazon: Barry wavy of four blue and white;
A robe of estate red, doubled ermine, its cord nowed and tassled gold.

Motto: By Luck And Good Guidance.

Date: 8.5.1943   **Frame:** Standard

Herald: Sir A. Cochrane

Derivation of Name:
Brecon, or to use its full name, the 'Brecon Farmers', is a foxhunt established in 1871. The pack, originally consisting of harrier hounds, was changed for foxhounds in 1906. The hunt country is totally within the borders of Brecon, Wales, and takes its name from the county town of the same name, which lies in the Usk valley.

Derivation of Badge:
The wavy field represents the river Usk which flows through the hunt country. The central charge of this badge, the robe (Mantle of Estate), has been adapted from the Arms of the Borough of Brecon, (or Brecknock); these in turn were derived from a seal, conjectured to have been granted to the town by Philip and Mary, in whose reign the town received its first Royal Charter in 1556.

Badge Heritage:
1. A 'Hunt Class Type IV* Escort Vessel built by Thornycroft, launched in 1942 and sold for scrapping in 1962.
2. A 'Hunt' Class Mine Countermeasures Vessel built by Vosper-Thornycroft and launched in 1978.

Notes:
* Only two of this Thornycroft design were built. With a hull form well in advance of their time, they were much more seaworthy ships than the earlier three types of 'Hunt' Class escorts.

MPL Neg. No.2011   circa 1946

June 1980

Blazon: Red; A castle of three towers its centre tower embattled and the outer round towers domed all silver, with portcullis gold, all upon a timber bridge of four braced piers also gold, in chief an estoile and a fleur-de-lys also gold.

Motto: Stet Fortuna Nostra. (May Our Fortune Stand.)

Date: 27.7.1928   **Frame:** Diamond

Herald: C. ffoulkes

Derivation of Name:
Confusion exists regarding the origin of this name but the writers are of the opinion that there was no connection originally with the town of Bridgwater, (note spelling), Somersetshire. Research suggests that this name was introduced into the Royal Navy in 1654 to honour John Egerton, created 1st Earl of Bridgewater on the 27th of May 1617. He was appointed Lord President of Wales and of the Marches in 1633 and died in 1649. The warship of 1928 (the fifth of this name) was one of a class of Sloops all named after coastal towns, but the spelling of the name was not changed to correspond with that of the town.

Derivation of Badge:
In 1928, the town of Bridgwater used Arms without grant based on an early seal of the town. The design of this badge is also taken from the same seal and coloured to follow the adopted Arms of the town.

Badge Heritage:
1. A 'Sandwich' Class Escort Sloop built by Hawthorn-Leslie, launched in 1928 and sold for scrapping in 1947.

Notes:
The anomaly of the spelling of the two names was pointed out by the town Council to the Admiralty, but no action was taken to correct it and sadly, the town forthwith refused to 'adopt' the ship.

The motto alludes to the bridge over the River Parret that connects both sides of the town.

MPL Neg. No.2443   May 1939

Blazon: Per fess wavy white and blue; in chief a rising sun radiant red, in fess three roses white, barbed and seeded proper.

Motto: Not recorded.

Date: 10.9.1940   **Frame:** Diamond

Herald: Sir A. Cochrane

Derivation of Name:
This name honours the town of Bridlington in the East Riding of Yorkshire. Bridlington Quay is the port for the town and provides a haven for small vessels in the harbour. The bay, protected by Flamborough Head and the Smethwick Sand during northerly gales, provides the only safe anchorage on the east coast between Harwich and Leith. This name was selected in 1939 for one of a class of Minesweepers all named after coastal towns of the United Kingdom.

Derivation of Badge:
The design of this badge is derived from various charges in the Arms of the Borough of Bridlington granted on the 27th of September 1934. The white and blue field with its wavy division line is from the chief of the Arms and refers to the coastal location of the town, whilst the red sun is taken from the Crest, as are the white roses.

(Bridlington employs a red sun in its Crest – to denote the many hours of sunshine the resort enjoys – shown rising from a 'coronet of York' – a circlet adorned with white roses.)

Badge Heritage:
1. A 'Bangor' Class Minesweeper built by Denny, launched in 1940, transferred to the Air Ministry in 1946 and eventually scrapped in 1958.

Notes:
Local legend has it that during the action off Flamborough Head in 1779 between H.M.S. Serapis and *Le Bon Homme Richard*, shots from the American squadron reached the shore at Bridlington.

W & L   circa 1941

Blazon: Barry wavy of six white and blue;
A castle white, between the towers a fleur-de-lys gold.

Motto: Not recorded.

Date: 10.9.1940   **Frame:** Diamond

Herald: Sir A. Cochrane

Derivation of Name:
Bridport is a town in south Dorsetshire on the river Brit, from which it takes its name. West Bay, a mile or so to the south, is the town's access to Lyme Bay and the sea. Since the 12th Century the town has been famous for the production of cable, nets, rope, and cordage for both the Royal Navy and merchant vessels, much of this rope being 'laid-up' in long, narrow back-garden 'ropewalks', a feature of many of the older houses. Much production of sail-cloth was also undertaken and the town is still one of the largest net-making centres in Europe. This name was selected in 1939 for one of a class of Minesweepers all named after coastal towns of the United Kingdom.

Derivation of Badge:
The field of wavy white and blue bars denotes equally the location of the town and the river Brit.

The castle with the fleur-de-lys placed above it has been adapted from the Arms of the town of Bridport as recorded in the Visitation of Heralds on the 3rd of October 1565.

Badge Heritage:
1. A 'Bangor' Class Minesweeper built by Denny*, launched in 1940 and transferred to the Air Ministry in 1946, being eventually scrapped in 1958.
2. A 'Sandown' Class Single Role Minehunter ordered from Vosper-Thornycroft in 1987.

Notes:
Denny only built two of this class (the other was H.M.S Bridlington) – their service careers and their eventual disposal was identical.

WSPL Kennedy Collection

1947

Blazon: White; A dolphin embowed black, charged with a hurt edged gold, thereon a mullet white.

Motto: Not recorded.

Date: 1.10.1941   **Frame:** Standard

Herald: Sir A. Cochrane

Derivation of Name:
Brighton, a coastal town in Sussex is the most fashionable resort in England and has many fine examples of Regency architecture. Before 1750, it was just a small village called Brighthelmstone, but rose to great popularity as a fashionable resort from the writings of Dr. Russell in the 18th Century, following the discovery of a chalybeate spring and particularly after the patronage of the Prince of Wales, who took an instant liking to the town whilst spending a holiday there in 1782 in the company of the Duke of Cumberland. The Prince built the Royal Pavilion in 1784 and took up a yearly residence in the town. This annual rest from his Court duties continued after his Coronation as King George IV in 1821. Brighton has always been connected with the fishing industry and its boats still bring in large numbers of herring and mackerel. After an absence from Navy Lists of some one hundred and sixty years this name was selected in 1940 for one of the ex-U.S. Navy destroyers transferred by the United States to Great Britain in exchange for sovereignty over certain overseas bases. These were all said to be named after towns and cities common to both countries. The town honoured by the name in the United States is thought to be the one in the State of Colorado* but cannot be stated for certain, as there are at least twelve towns of the name in that country.

Derivation of Badge:
The design for this badge is derived from the Arms granted to the County Borough of Brighton on the 14th of April 1897. These Arms include two black dolphins on a field of argent – the badge shows one of them on a white field (argent). The military emblem of the United States has been placed on the dolphin to denote that the ship is one of the fifty destroyers transferred from the United States to Great Britain in 1940. This emblem is edged in gold to separate the blue from the black, in accordance with Heraldic convention.

Badge Heritage:
1. A 'Town' Class Destroyer built by Fore River, launched in 1918 and served in the U.S. Navy as the *U.S.S. Cowell*. She was transferred to the Royal Navy and renamed H.M.S. Brighton in 1940. She was on loan to the Russian Navy from 1944 until 1949 and served as the *Zharki*. She was sold for scrapping in 1949.
2. A 'Rothesay' Class Frigate built by Yarrow, launched in 1959 and sold for scrapping in 1985.

Notes:
* Research is continuing on this question, as mentioned earlier in this volume.

IWM Neg. No.A9220   circa 1943

Navpic   1st October 1979

Blazon: Black; An annulet radiant of twelve points gold.

Motto: Ea Nostra Vocamus. (We Claim The Deeds Of Our Ancestors.)

Date: 4.7.1929   **Frame:** Shield

Herald: C. ffoulkes

Derivation of Name:
This name was introduced into the Royal Navy by the capture of the French Sloop *Brilliant*, in 1696. The word 'brilliant' means brightly shining, glittering, sparkling or lustrous.

Derivation of Badge:
The design is derived from the badge of the seventh ship of this name, a 2nd Class Cruiser, which participated in the action at Ostend on the 23rd of April 1918, when she was sunk as a blockship in an unsuccessful attempt to deny the harbour to the occupying German forces.

That badge had the letter 'B' within a ring surrounded by twelve rays. Mr. ffoulkes modified this design by removing the letter 'B', altering the shape of the twelve rays and leaving the centre of the ring a plain flat surface. This was to give an alternative meaning to the word 'brilliant', namely a diamond of the finest cut. In the diamond trade a brilliant has horizontal faces on its upper and lower side, which

are surrounded and united by facets. This design shows therefore, the 'table' of a diamond within its setting and surrounded by rays. The use of black as a field colour also has more than one meaning. Firstly, it may mourn the loss of life at Zeebrugge and Ostend in April 1918, but more importantly, it is also another reference to a diamond. In Heraldry, it was formerly a fashion to blazon the Arms of Royalty and nobles by jewels. Black, blazoned by jewels, is diamond.

Badge Heritage:
1. A 'B' Class Destroyer built by Swan Hunter, launched in 1930 and sold for scrapping in 1947.
2. A Type 22 Frigate, built by Yarrow and launched in 1978.*

Notes:
* The badge for this ship was re-carved for a Standard Circular frame in the Pattern Shop, Devonport in 1984, but due to an error it no longer holds the original significance of the name. No record existed as to the derivation of the badge and it was wrongly assumed to be representative of a sun, because a badge of this design was sent from the builders to Devonport. The ship's badge was carved accordingly, with the flat in the centre filled with a semi-circular sphere. It is to be hoped that the Commanding Officer of the present ship will be permitted to make due representation for the supply of a correct badge to maintain the link of his ship with her predecessors, particularly when the motto is borne in mind.

W & L   July 1931

Navpic   5th June 1981

Blazon: Green; A hare sejant affrontee proper.

Motto: Not recorded.

Date: 17.10.1942   **Frame:** Standard

Herald: Sir A. Cochrane

Derivation of Name:
Brissenden, more correctly the 'Brissenden Beagles', is a hunt in Kent that takes its name from a small hamlet to the south-west of Ashford. The pack, privately owned, was previously called the Betherden and later the Oakhurst beagles, before being renamed with its present title by its owner, Lt.-Col. H. C. Hessey in 1937*.

Derivation of Badge:
The design for this badge was suggested by Lt.-Col. Hessey – the field colour to represent the 'Beagle green' of the uniform coat of the hunt, and the alert hare as the quarry of the huntsmen.

Badge Heritage:
1. A 'Hunt' Class Type IV Escort Vessel built by Thornycroft, launched in 1942 and sold for scrapping in 1965.

Notes:
* These details are given as they would have applied in 1940 when the name was allocated, for the pack was disbanded early in World War II and not reformed.

MOD(N)   10th February 1943

Blazon: Red; Issuant from the sinister side and barry wavy of five in base blue and white, a castle embattled proper, flotant to sinister from its domed tower a pennon white, charged with a cross red, emerging from its port blue, with portcullis raised gold, an ancient ship with a mast all gold, rigging and sail set white.

Motto: Not recorded.

Date: 14.2.1969   **Frame:** Standard

Herald: Capt. E. M. C. Barraclough R.N.

Derivation of Name:
Bristol is a cathedral City and an ancient seaport, the city proper being in Gloucestershire, though some of its suburbs are in Somerset. At one time it was the first seaport in Christendom, and the atmosphere in the early seafaring days was well captured by R. L. Stevenson's 'Treasure Island'. The city owed its greatness to seaborne trade and the Bristol Merchant Venturer's Association was formed in 1552. The *Great Western* was launched here in 1837, followed by the *Great Britain* in 1843. Bristol's seaborne trade is now overshadowed by nearby Avonmouth Docks, but it remains nevertheless a major commercial centre of the West of England.

Derivation of Badge:
This simplified design is based on the Arms of the City of Bristol recorded and confirmed on the 24th of August 1569. These Arms are traceable, in turn, to a 14th Century seal of the Mayoralty, which refers to the castle with a concealed port, through which merchant ships were able to pass to and from the City on their lawful occasions.

Badge Heritage:
1. A Type 82* Destroyer built by Swan Hunter and launched in 1969.

Notes:
* Eight ships of this class were originally envisaged, but only four were ordered, and three of these were subsequently cancelled.

October 1972

Blazon: Per fess wavy blue, and barry wavy of four white and blue;
An increscent gold, overall a net disposed bendwise black.

Motto: Not recorded.

Date: 15.5.1938   **Frame:** Diamond

Herald: Sir A. Cochrane

Derivation of Name:
This name is of literary origin and is a character from Spencer's 'Faerie Queene'. In this work Britomart, a female knight, is the daughter of King Ryence of Wales and is the personification of chastity and purity who eventually marries Artegal.

Derivation of Badge:
For the purpose of the badge design, the derivation was said to be from Britomartis, a Cretan nymph of Greek mythology, the daughter of Zeus and Carme. She was brought into the cult of Artemis and made one of her attendants. Like Artemis, she was known as Dictynna in Crete, and this name, (which means the Lady of the Nets), is explained by the legend that whilst being pursued by Minos, she threw herself into the sea from the clifftops, but was saved by being caught in a fisherman's net. She then fled to Aegina where she was worshipped as Aphaia (the invisible). The design shows an increscent for Britomartis in her identification with Artemis (associated with the moon), and a net for her, in her alias as Dictynna, placed on a field of the sea from which she was plucked.

Badge Heritage:
1. A 'Halcyon' Class Fleet Minesweeper built by H.M. Dockyard, Devonport and launched in 1938. She was sunk in very tragic circumstances on the 27th of August 1944, off Cape d'Antifer. Whilst under the command of Lieut.-Cdr. J. A. Galvin D.S.C., R.D., R.N.R., she was attacked in error by Typhoon aircraft of the 2nd Tactical Air Force,* with the loss of two officers and twenty ratings. Cdr. Galvin was one of the officers killed.

Notes:
* During this incident, H.M.S. Hussar, under the command of Lieut. R. Nash M.B.E., R.N.R., was also attacked and sunk with the loss of three officers and fifty-three ratings, H.M.S. Jason, under the command of Cdr. T. Crick D.S.C., R.N., was damaged with the loss of two ratings, H.M.S. Salamander, under the command of Lieut.-Cdr. H. King R.N.V.R., was damaged beyond repair; the trawlers H.M.T. Colsay and H.M.T. Lord Ashfield were also damaged. An enquiry revealed that a vital signal giving the presence of these ships in the area had not been repeated to Flag Officer British Assault Area from Captain (M), consequently they were thought to be German ships and an air strike was ordered. No blame can be attached to the R.A.F. for this incident.

MOD(N)   31st December 1941

Blazon: White; An anchor bendwise to sinister and a trawl-bar in saltire all black.

Motto: Not recorded.

Date: 7.7.1942   **Frame:** Standard

Herald: Sir A. Cochrane

Derivation of Name:
Brixham* is a seaport in Devonshire, irregularly built on cliffs to the south of Torbay, with its harbour sheltered by a breakwater. It is the centre of the fishing industry of Torbay and was known as the 'Mother of the sea-fishing industry', because Brixham fishermen invented and developed the trawling system of catching fish, which enabled bottom-swimming fish to be harvested – a catch Drifters were unable to net. The method entailed towing a cone-shaped net across the sea-bed, its mouth being stretched open by a long trawl 'head' or beam. This system was improved in the 1890s by the substitution of otter-boards, which performed the same task.

Derivation of Badge:
The design shows a representation of a trawl-beam to signify Brixham's main industry, on an anchor to denote its maritime connections.

Badge Heritage:
1. A 'Bangor' Class Fleet Minesweeper built by Blyth Shipbuilding, launched in 1941 and sold for scrapping in 1948.

Notes:
The National Maritime Museum's Sea Fishing museum and the National Coastguard museum can both be visited at Brixham.
   * As an historical footnote, Brixham was the landfall made by William of Orange on the 5th of November 1689, and the town motto – 'The Liberties Of England I Will Maintain' – was originally spoken by him.

IWM Neg. No.FL2982   circa 1941

Blazon: Barry wavy of eight white and blue;
A torteau, surmounted by a broadsword its point in base proper.

Motto: Not recorded.

Date: 13.3.1946   **Frame:** Standard

Herald: Sir A. Cochrane

Derivation of Name:
A broadsword is a large double-edged cutting sword that derives its name from its broad blade. This weapon was thought to have been introduced by the Vikings and from this in turn was developed the 'Great Sworde' of the medieval era.

Derivation of Badge:
The sword shown in the badge is a Saxon broadsword and it is shown point downwards to indicate that there is no allusion in the charge, other than the charge itself. It is on a roundel, coloured red to symbolise martialism, which is in turn placed upon a field of wavy white and blue to denote the sea. The design thus gives an illustration of the name.

Badge Heritage:
1. A 'Weapon' Class Destroyer built by Yarrow, launched in 1946 and sold for scrapping in 1968.
2. A Type 22 Frigate built by Yarrow and launched in 1976.

Notes:
As this design is the last one for a Type 22 Frigate to be described in this volume, it is appropriate to mention the badge 'that never was' for one of this class 'that never was'! The eighth ship of this class to be ordered was to be named H.M.S. Bloodhound and was allocated the badge of H.M.S. Hound, appearing as such on a R.N. Recruiting poster of ship's badges in 1984. This was directly opposed to one of the first guidelines of official badges that no two ship names would wear the same badge. However, as this ship was renamed H.M.S. London following depositions from the City, (and launched as such), this anomaly resolved itself.

W & L   March 1949

W & L   February 1983

Blazon: Red; The Pelham buckle palewise gold.

Motto: Love Of Country Conquers.*

Date: 1.12.1942   **Frame:** Standard

Herald: Sir A. Cochrane

Derivation of Name:
The 'Brocklesby' is a foxhunt that derives its name from Brocklesby Park, near Ulceby, Lincolnshire. It is the pack belonging to the distinguished family of Pelham, the Earls of Yarborough. Founded circa 1700, its Mastership was held by a member of this family from its establishment, up until 1939.

Brocklesby Park is the family seat of the Pelhams and has been so since the 16th Century.

Derivation of Badge:
This design is derived from the Arms of Pelham, which are: red; two pieces of belt with buckles erect. The badge also uses red as a field colour, additionally to denote the colour of the hunt uniform. The buckle is from a sword-belt, originally adopted by Sir John de Pelham as a badge to mark his part in the capture of the French King John at Poictiers in 1356 and is used in the badge to emphasise the family of Pelham's connection with the hunt.

Badge Heritage:
1. A 'Hunt' Class Type II Escort Vessel built by Cammell Laird, launched in 1940 and sold for scrapping in 1968**.
2. A 'Hunt' Class Mine Counter Measures Vessel built by Vosper-Thornycroft and launched in 1982.

Notes:
* This motto, a variation of the family motto of the Pelhams, (Vincit Amor Patriae, The Love Of My Country Prevails), was not used by the first ship to wear the badge.

**This ship was the longest-serving of the 'Hunt' class in the Royal Navy, due to her long use as an Asdic Trials and Training Ship.

MOD(N)   1942

Navpic   13th June 1987

Blazon: White; A dexter cubit arm erect proper, the hand holding a trident bendwise to sinister gold, all between two branches of laurel conjoined in base proper, banded and fructed gold.

Motto: Seavum Tridentum Servanus. (Let Us Keep The Dread Trident.)

Date: 9.5.1923   **Frame:** Shield

Herald: C. ffoulkes

Derivation of Name:
This name perpetuates the memory of Rear-Admiral Sir Philip Bowes Vere Broke (1776-1841). Entering the Royal Navy in 1792, he first saw active service in the Mediterranean from 1793 until 1795 and participated in the battle of Cape St. Vincent in 1797 and also took part in the defeat and capture of the French fleet off Ireland in 1798. He was promoted to the rank of Captain in 1801 and in 1806 he was appointed in command of H.M.S. Shannon. During the War of Independence between Great Britain and the United States, it was whilst commanding this ship that he fought the action for which he is best remembered. On the 1st of June 1813, off Boston, Mass., he engaged and captured the *U.S.S. Chesapeake* after a bloody encounter of less than fifteen minutes duration. Capt.

Broke was severely wounded leading a boarding party against the American ship, (which incapacitated him from further active service and for the rest of his life caused him serious suffering), but for this action he was awarded a Naval Gold Medal, and created a Baronet in 1813. He was made a K.C.B. in 1815, promoted to Rear-Admiral in 1830 and died in London on the 2nd of January 1841.

Derivation of Badge:
The design of this badge is the Crest of the Arms of Admiral Broke, placed on a white field to provide contrast.

Badge Heritage:
1. A 'Shakespeare' Class Destroyer Leader built by Thornycroft and launched in 1920 as H.M.S. Rooke. She was renamed H.M.S. Broke* in 1921 and completed in H.M. Dockyard, Portsmouth. She was lost whilst participating in the landing at Algiers on the 8th of November 1942, sinking after sustaining heavy damage from Vichy French shore batteries, with the loss of nine ratings.

Notes:
* Research has not yielded the reason for this change. The motto is also that of Admiral Broke.

Blazon: Gold; A saltire red, charged with a spider gold.

Motto: Tentata Attingo. (By Attempt I Attain.)

Date: 27.9.1919   **Frame:** Shield

Herald: C. ffoulkes

Derivation of Name:
This name commemorates Robert 'The Bruce', (1274-1329), King Robert I of Scotland. Rightful heir to the throne of Scotland, and denied his accession by Edward I, his attempts to obtain his inheritance were at first unsuccessful. His fortunes reached their nadir at Methven when he was defeated in a surprise attack by the Lord of Norn; his wife and his daughter were captured, and his brother Nigel, together with many of his supporters, were executed as traitors.

He was forced to withdraw from Scotland and wintered on the island of Rathlin, off the north coast of Ireland. In 1307 Bruce landed at Turnberry, Ayrshire, defeating the Earl of Pembroke. The campaign was completely successful and final victory was ensured at the battle of Bannockburn in 1314. He reigned until his death in 1329.*

The name was selected in 1917 for one of a class of Destroyer Leaders all named after Scottish Clan Chiefs.

Derivation of Badge:
The red cross on its gold field is from the Arms of Robert I. Legend relates that it was whilst the down-hearted Bruce was on Rathlin Island contemplating his fate, he observed a spider struggling to build its web. It tried many times to secure the web before it was eventually successful – Bruce took this as an omen and resolved to try again. The spider in the badge records this legend.

Badge Heritage:
1. A 'Scott' Class Destroyer Leader, built by Cammell Laird, launched in 1918, and expended as a target in 1939.
2. A Shore Establishment at Crail, Scotland commissioned in 1947 and paid off in 1949.

Notes:
The motto recalls the legend of the spider.

*By his will, his heart was to be buried in Jerusalem. It was entrusted to Sir James Douglas but he was killed in 1330 fighting against the Moors in Spain, whilst en route to the Holy Land. The heart was later recovered from the battlefield and is interred in the High Altar in Melrose Abbey.

MPL Neg. No.1703   1927

Blazon: Green; A bryony leaf environed by its tendrils flowered and seeded all gold.

Motto: Floreo Dum Vigilo. (I Flourish Whilst I Watch.)

Date: 21.4.1933 **Frame:** Diamond

Herald: C. ffoulkes

Derivation of Name:
The byrony, *Bryonia dioica*, is a species of wild flower. It is a tall climbing perennial of hedgerows and sandy soil, with clinging tendrils rising from the bristly stems close to the ivy-shaped leaves.

The name was selected in 1916 for one of a class of Sloops all named after flowers.

Derivation of Badge:
The use of green for the field of this badge is to denote the habitat of the flower. The flower itself, coloured gold is an heraldic interpretation, and the complete design is expressive of the meaning of the name.

Badge Heritage:
1. A 'Flower' Class, (Anchusa Group), Sloop built by Armstrong. launched in 1917 and sold for scrapping in 1938.

Notes:
The motto refers to the fact that in flower 'language', the Bryony symbolises prosperity and also to the Fishery Protection duty undertaken by this ship.

Blazon: Gold; A lion's head erazed black, langued red, in its mouth a battleaxe bendwise to sinister black.

Motto: Not recorded.

Date: 13.3.1946　　**Frame:** Standard

Herald: Sir A. Cochrane

Derivation of Name:
Buchan Ness is the most easterly cape of Scotland and is located three miles from Peterhead, Aberdeenshire. It has a lighthouse upon its summit, built by Robert Stevenson, brother of George Stevenson. Nearby are the Bullers of Buchan, an enormous rocky cavern into which waves pour through a natural arch of granite, with incredible violence during a storm.

Derivation of Badge:
The gold field denotes Scotland as it is both the field colour of its Arms and its Standard. The black lion's head is derived from the Arms of the Earl of Buchan to record that the Highland province in which Buchan Ness lies was ruled by the Pictish Mormaers of Buchan, who subsequently emerged as the Earls of Buchan in the 12th Century. This was the most powerful and ancient Earldom in the Highlands, and consequently much fought over. This is thought to be the allusion of the black battleaxe in the mouth of the lion.*

Badge Heritage:
1. A Depot Ship for Landing Craft built by West Coast Shipbuilders, launched in 1945 and sold for scrapping in 1959.

Notes:
* An alternative name for Buchan Ness, now disused, was Boddam Point. The word 'boden' means 'equipped or accoutred'. Is this lion 'boden' for war?

W & L

February 1946

Blazon: Blue; A saltire couped white, surmounted by a trident black.

Motto: Not recorded.

Date: 31.1.1942   **Frame:** Standard

Herald: Sir A. Cochrane

Derivation of Name:
Bude is a town on the north coast of Cornwall and is located at the mouth of a river of the same name. It faces the full force of the Atlantic rollers and gales on a coast formerly notorious for wreckers and ship-wrecks. With the town of Stratton one and a half miles inland, it forms the Urban District of Stratton and Bude.

Bude's modern castle was built in 1830 by Sir Goldsworthy Gurney, the noted Cornish inventor, who was responsible for a light that bears the name of the town, which was the forerunner of a much improved type of lighthouse.

Derivation of Badge:
The parish church of Stratton and Bude is that of St. Andrew's, built in 1348. St. Andrew's distinguishing cross is the white saltire, and this has been used in the design to allude to the location of the town. The trident is frequently used as a symbol of Naval sea-power and is thought to be presented black to denote mourning for the many lives of seamen lost over the years in the numerous wrecks that took place here.*

Badge Heritage:
1. A 'Bangor' Class Minesweeper built by Lobnitz Shipbuilders, launched in 1940 and sold for scrapping in 1946.

Notes:
* Graves of many of these seamen may be seen in the churchyard and also the figurehead of the East India-man *Bencoolen*, a brig of 1,415 tons, wrecked on the sands near Bude on the 19th of October 1862, with the loss of twenty-six of her crew. Many other vessels were lost during this great storm.

Blazon: Gold; A male African elephant statant in reeds its trunk held aloft all proper.

Motto: Sustain The Fight.

Date: 24.11.1947   **Frame:** Standard

Herald: Sir A. Cochrane

Derivation of Name:
Bulawayo is the capital city of Matabeleland, the Western Province of Southern Rhodesia. The name, translated from the Zulu language means 'the place of slaughter'. Founded in 1893 by the British South Africa Company, it occupies the central area of a 4,500 foot high tableland. The Zulu interpretation of the name was forcibly brought home in March 1896, when the Matabele under their chief, Olimo, rebelled. Two hundred and fifty-seven settlers were massacred.

Derivation of Badge:
The gold field is thought to denote that the surrounding area of the City is crossed by numerous gold "reefs". The elephant in reeds is derived from the Crest of the Arms of the City and this animal, according to some authorities, was also a symbol of the Matabele nation.

Perhaps coincidentally, the elephant standing in reeds yields a partial pun on the name, as the animal is a male — a bull elephant; whilst reeds are an Heraldic term for Bulrushes.

Badge Heritage:
1. An Oiler, previously the German *Nordmark*, seized in 1945 and renamed R.F.A. Northmark. She was renamed H.M.S. Bulawayo* in 1947 and sold for scrapping in 1955.

Notes:
* The Rhodesian High Commission requested in 1944 that a ship be named H.M.S. Bulawayo. No suitable vessel was available until 1945 when it was decided to allocate this name to one of the 'A' class batch of Submarines, whose names were all to begin with the letter 'B'. However, the batch was cancelled, and this ship was the first available.

Blazon: Black; A bulldog statant affrontee white.*

Motto: Hold Fast.

Date: 18.8.1929   **Frame:** Shield

Herald: C. ffoulkes

Derivation of Name:
This is a breed of dog, probably a sub-variety of the mastiff crossed with lesser breeds and, as its name indicates, was originally employed for the baiting of bulls. In Elizabethan times, these dogs were perhaps the most sought-after English breed, because of the prevalence of the sports of bull- and bear-baiting. Their ability to seize and cling to the animals they baited became proverbial, due in part to their innate courage, and partly to the fact that the 'underbite', or locked jaw, peculiar to the breed makes it difficult for them to release their hold. During the 18th and 19th Centuries the breed was in high favour because of its fighting abilities.

Derivation of Badge:
This design was suggested by the Director of Naval Equipment, Vice-Admiral J. W. Henley R.N. The badge shows a white bulldog, this being the colour of the 'standard' English bulldog. The use of black is thought to indicate that the design was for a Destroyer. This field colour was frequently used for early destroyer designs and where no other allusion was intended it is thought that it was in reference to the fact that Destroyers were originally painted black.**

Badge Heritage:
1. A 'B' Class Destroyer built by Swan Hunter, launched in 1930 and sold for scrapping in 1946.
2. A Survey Vessel built by Brooke Marine and launched in 1967.

Notes:
The motto denotes the renowned grip of the bulldog.

 * The blazon given here corresponds with the sealed pattern and not as the badge was carved. In the carving the bulldog's body is more in profile and is a much sturdier animal than the one drawn.

 ** This tends to be confirmed by the fact that this is precisely why the fields of the name panels for Destroyer badges were originally painted black.

 As a curious footnote, this badge is identical to the Formation Sign used by the famed 6th Corps of the British Army commanded by Lt.-Gen. Sir James Haldane during the First World War. One cannot help but wonder if this was the inspiration for this design.

MPL Neg. No.1885   July 1935

W & L   September 1979

Blazon: Barry wavy of ten white and blue;
A sword silver, with grip black, the blade enfiled by a palisado crown gold.

Motto: Under Thy Wings I Will Trust.

Date: 2.4.1947   **Frame:** Standard

Herald: Sir A. Cochrane

Derivation of Name:
The word 'bulwark' is probably of Scandinavian origin and originally meant a fortification or barricade constructed of logs. The word gradually became a general expression of anything serving as a defence. It also means the raised ship's side, above the level of the upper decks.

Derivation of Badge:
The badge shows a sword, symbolic of military might, within a crown in the form of a palisade*.

This is in allusion to the name, as a palisade is also a fortification or a barricade made of stakes. The two charges are depicted on a field representing the sea to denote that this is a 'naval bulwark'.

Badge Heritage:
1. A 'Hermes' Class Light Fleet Carrier built by Harland & Wolff, launched in 1948 and sold for scrapping in 1984.

Notes:
* This crown (Latin – *'Corona Castrensis'* or *'Corona Vallaris'*) was awarded in Roman times to the first soldier to surmount the bulwark and force an entrance into the enemy's camp.

It is on record that King John I of England (1167-1216) described England as 'That water-walled Bulwark still secure and confident from Foreign purposes.'

The motto refers to the protection afforded by the aircraft embarked in the ship.

Blazon: Per fess wavy gold, and barry wavy of four white and blue;
Issuant from fess four piles inverted conjoined green.

Motto: Not recorded.

Date: 23.2.1953   **Frame:** Standard

Herald: Sir A. Cochrane

Derivation of Name:
Burghead Bay is at the mouth of the Moray Firth off the coast between Findhorn and Burghead, in the county of Moray, Scotland. When the Romans made their circumnavigation of Britain in 86 A.D., this rockbound peninsula would have been an outstanding feature of their exploration. Ptolemy, the geographer, who drew up a chart of the island from their observations, notes in this region what the sailors described as a 'Winged Camp', (*Alata castra*).

Derivation of Badge:
The field of gold denotes that the bay is located in Scotland, (the Arms and Standard of Scotland both have a gold field.) The piles are an Heraldic expression of hills and are shown with a representation of the sea at their feet. These piles 'indicate the four Roman hills upon which the town of Burghead stands'.*

Badge Heritage:
1. A 'Bay' Class Frigate built by Hill, launched in 1945 and transferred to the Portuguese Navy in 1959 as the *Alvares Cabral*.

Notes:
For an explanation of the long delay between the launch of this ship and the grant of her badge, please see the notes for H.M.S. Bamborough Castle.
   * MOD(N) records state that the piles are in allusion to the four Roman hills upon which the town of Burghead stands, (PR.7000/52), but this is not correct. The peninsula upon which Burghead stands is flat and although the identity of Burghead with the *Alata Castra* of Ptolemy is fairly certain, whether the Romans actually landed there, strengthening its defences and forming a northern outpost of their Empire, has become a matter of dispute. The most prominent feature from any part of Burghead Bay is the shoreline of Sutherland and Caithness on the other side of the Moray Firth and visible upon it are four distinct peaks.

Skyfotos Neg. No.10276

June 1953

Blazon: Per fess wavy blue, and barry wavy of three white and blue;
Three torches, one erect two is saltire gold, enflamed proper, surmounted by a hurt thereon a mullet white.

Motto: Not recorded.

Date: 11.11.1941   **Frame:** Standard

Herald: Sir A. Cochrane

Derivation of Name:
This name was selected in 1940 for one of the fifty destroyers transferred to the Royal Navy from the United States.* The names of these ships were said to be in honour of towns common to both the United States and Great Britain. It cannot be stated with certainty which town in the United Kingdom is honoured as there are several of this name, but our research leads us to believe that it is Burnham-on-Sea, Somerset. It is thought that the town selected in the United States is the one in the State of Maine.

Derivation of Badge:
The design of this badge yields the evidence for the identity of the English town. The field is divided in half and one half represents the sea. Three burning torches complete the allusion to the name (Burn 'em on sea – Burnham-on-sea). The torches have a representation of the military emblem of the United States placed upon them, to denote the origin of the ship.

Badge Heritage:
1. A 'Town' Class Destroyer built by Bethlehem, launched in 1919 and served in the U.S. Navy as the *U.S.S. Aulick*. She was transferred to the Royal Navy in 1940 and renamed H.M.S. Burnham. She was sold for scrapping in 1948.

Notes:
* This name was first selected during the First World War for a Minesweeper but was not taken up.

IWM Neg. No.FL3198

circa 1941

Blazon: Barry wavy of six white and blue;
A thistle slipped leaved and flowered proper, its stalk surmounted by a hurt thereon a mullet white.

Motto: Not recorded.

Date: 1.10.1941   **Frame:** Standard

Herald: Sir A. Cochrane

Derivation of Name:
This name was selected in 1940 for one of the fifty destroyers transferred to the Royal Navy from the United States. They were said to be named after towns common to the United States of America and the United Kingdom.

Burwell, in England, is a town in Cambridgeshire, four miles north-west of Newmarket. Within its boundaries stand the ruins of a castle, built prior to the Norman Conquest and a beautiful Gothic church. Burwell, in the U.S.A., is a city and county seat of Garfield County, Central Nebraska, north-west of Grand Island. It was settled in the 1880s and serves as the marketing centre for the large surrounding cattle area.

Derivation of Badge:
This design is a partial pun on the name and shows a thistle or 'burr' on a field representing the sea. On the stalk of the thistle is a representation of the military emblem of the United States of America, used to denote the origin of the ship.

Badge Heritage:
1. A 'Town' Class Destroyer built by Bethlehem, launched in 1918 and served in the U.S. Navy as *U.S.S. Laub*. She was transferred to the Royal Navy and renamed H.M.S. Burwell in 1940 and sold for scrapping in 1947.

Notes:
On the 28th of August 1941 H.M.S. Burwell took part in the capture of *U-570*, surrendered the previous day to a Hudson aircraft of 269 Sqn R.A.F. *U-570* was subsequently commissioned into the Royal Navy as H.M.S. Graph and was lost in 1944.

IWM Neg. No.FL3199

circa 1942

Blazon: Blue; A buck's head caboshed white, between its attires a mullet also white.

Motto: Not recorded.

Date: 15.10.1941   **Frame:** Standard

Herald: Sir A. Cochrane

Derivation of Name:
This name was introduced into the Royal Navy in 1940 for one of the fifty destroyers transferred from the United States to the Royal Navy in exchange for sovereignty of certain overseas bases, mainly in the West Indies. They were said to be named after towns common to both countries.

Buxton, in England, is a town in the Peak District in the County of Derbyshire. It is renowned for its natural hot springs and possesses many fine buildings including a handsome pumproom. Most of these buildings owe their existence to the town's patron, William Cavendish (1748-1811), 5th Duke of Devonshire. He was also responsible for the hospital that bears his title (Devonshire), several schools and a lending library.

Buxton, in the United States, cannot be clearly identified as there are four towns of the name in that country.

Derivation of Badge:
This badge design is partially inspired by the Crest of the Arms of Buxton. This Crest is a buck, 'at gaze', in its proper colours and the designer has used only its head to provide the central charge of the badge. It is coloured white to give a pun on the name of the town, i.e. a 'stone buck' or 'buckstone'. An additional allusion is made by the use of this design, namely to William Cavendish, the town's benefactor. His Arms were three buck's heads argent (white) on a blue field. The white star denotes the origin of the ship and is presented without its normal blue roundel as the field is blue.

Badge Heritage:
1. A 'Town' Class Destroyer built by Bethlehem, launched in 1918 and served in the U.S. Navy as the *U.S.S. Edwards*. She was transferred to the Royal Navy in 1940 as H.M.S. Buxton and then to the Royal Canadian Navy in 1943 who disposed of her in 1945.

Notes:
This ship was adopted by the town of Buxton, Derbyshire in 1941 and, to mark the association, a replica of the town's Arms was presented to the ship.

IWM Neg. No.FL3202   circa 1942

Blazon: Green; Above barry wavy of two in base white, and blue, a buzzard affrontee volant proper.

Motto: Not recorded.

Date: 11.6.1940   **Frame:** Standard

Herald: Sir A. Cochrane

Derivation of Name:
Buzzard is the name applied to birds of prey belonging to the sub-family *Buteoninae*. They are distinguished by their rather slow and heavy flight, the short rounded head, *Buteo vulgaris*, is now rare as a breeding species in Britain, but is widely distributed over the globe.

This name was selected in 1938 for a Fleet Air Arm Air Station.*

Derivation of Badge:
The use of green in the field denotes the country habitat of the bird, with water in base denoting the coast, as Lympne is a coastal airfield. The bird is depicted proper. The design illustrates the name and gives a clue to the location of the base.

Badge Heritage:
1. An F.A.A. Station at Lympne, Kent commissioned in 1939 and paid off in 1940.
2. An F.A.A. Station at Kingston, Jamaica, commissioned in 1940 and paid off in 1944.

Notes:
* Most F.A.A. Stations were, (and still are), named after birds.

Fleet Air Arm Museum

MISCELLANEOUS BADGE DETAILS

During the course of our research, we discovered details of two badges that do not have either a sealed pattern or a listing in the records of carvings held at Devonport Pattern Shop. As this work must strictly confine itself to detailing only official badges where a sealed pattern or a carving is known to exist (or known to have existed), we have not included details of these two badges in our main listing.

The writers feel that there was a definite intention to use one if the designated ship had not been transferred. The other was definitely designed by Charles ffoulkes, but was withdrawn because it was decided that this type of ship would not be granted a badge. They are listed below for record purposes.

H.M.S. BISHOPSGATE

Blazon: Red; A gateway gold over wavelets silver and blue.

Motto: Nisi Dominus Frustra. (Without The Lord In Vain.)
This is a variant of the City of London motto: Domine Dirige Nos.

Explanation of Badge:
From Thornbury and Walford's 'History of London'.

This pattern would have been dated circa 1930 and the designated ship was a Gate Vessel, built by Robb, launched in 1932 and sold for scrapping in 1959. The ship was one of a class all named after famous London gates. A note recorded in the minutes of the Ship's Badges Committee reads as follows: 'Gate Vessels – Not to have badges designed or supplied. NS6606/35'. This note is in the handwriting of Mr. D. Bonner-Smith, Admiralty Librarian and Secretary of the Committee.

Details of badge designs for two others of this class (Dowgate and Ludgate) also appear in Admiralty records.

This pattern was designed by C. ffoulkes and it appears in his listings, but no further details are known.

MOD(N)   Photograph taken 1933

H.M.S. BATH

Blazon: Barry wavy of six white and blue;
A sword in pale point upwards red, pommel and hilt gold, enfiled by a mural crown white, thereon a hurt charged with a mullet white.

Explanation of Badge:
Based on the recorded Arms of the City of Bath. The (hurt and) mullet signify that this was one of the Destroyers transferred to the Royal Navy by the U.S.A.

The design is shown in the Memorial windows of St Georges Church at the former Royal Naval Barracks, Chatham, where all Chatham-manned ships lost during World War II are commemorated, (also curious, as records confirm that at the time of her loss she was manned by the Royal Norwegian Navy). It is thought that this badge was designed by Sir A. Cochrane sometime in 1940 but was not used because of her transfer to the Norwegians in January 1941. (She was only commissioned into the R.N. in October 1940.) The details of the blazon and explanation as given appear in Ship's Badges Committee records.

CARVINGS

Patterns Carved for H.M. Dockyard, Chatham 1921-1982

Name	Screen Badge	Boat Badge	Name	Screen Badge	Boat Badge
Bacchante	1 (ST)	2 (ST)	Boston	1 (ST)	Nil
Bacchus	1 (P)	Nil	Boxer	1 (ST)	Nil
Badsworth	1 (ST)	Nil	Boyne	1 (A)	2 (A)
Bamborough Castle	1 (ST)	Nil	Bradford	1 (ST)	Nil
Bangor	1 (A)	Nil	Bramble	1 (A)	1 (A)
Barfleur	1 (ST)	Nil	Bramham	1 (ST)	Nil
Barham	1 (BS)	4 (BS)	Brave	1 (ST)	Nil
Barrosa	1 (ST)	Nil	Brazen	1 (D)	1 (D)
Basilisk	1 (D)	2 (D)	Brecon	1 (ST)	Nil
Basset	1 (A)	2 (A)	Bridgewater	1 (A)	1 (A)
Bastion	1 (ST)	Nil	Bridlington	1 (A)	Nil
Battleaxe	1 (ST)	2 (ST)	Bridport	1 (A)	Nil
Battler	1 (ST)	Nil	Brighton	1 (ST)	2 (ST)
Bayleaf	1 (P)	1 (P)	Brilliant	1 (D)	1 (D)
Beachy Head	1 (ST)	Nil	Brissenden	1 (ST)	Nil
Beagle	1 (D)	2 (D)	Bristol	1 (ST)	1 (ST)
Beatty	1 (BS)	2 (BS)	Britomart	1 (A)	2 (A)
Beaufort (1st)	1 (A)	2 (A)	Britannia	1	2
Beaufort (2nd)	1 (ST)	Nil	Brixham	1 (ST)	Nil
Beauly Firth	1 (ST)	Nil	Broadsword	1 (ST)	Nil
Beaumaris	1 (ST)	Nil	Brocklesby	1 (ST)	Nil
Bedale	1 (ST)	Nil	Broke	1 (D)	2 (D)
Bedouin	1 (D)	2 (D)	Bruce	1 (D)	1 (D)
Bee	1 (A), 1 (ST)	4 (A)	Bryony	1 (A)	2 (A)
Begum	1 (ST)	Nil	Buchan Ness	1 (ST)	Nil
Belfast	1 (P)	4 (P)	Bude	1 (ST)	Nil
Bellerophon	1 (ST)	Nil	Bulawayo	1 (ST)	Nil
Bellona	1 (ST)	Nil	Bulldog	1 (D)	2 (D)
Belmont	1 (ST)	Nil	Bulwark	1 (ST)	1 (ST)
Belvoir	1 (ST)	Nil	Burghead Bay	1 (ST)	Nil
Benbow	1 (BS)	4 (BS)	Burnham	1 (ST)	Nil
Ben Lomond	1 (ST)	Nil	Burwell	1 (ST)	Nil
Berkeley	1 (A)	1 (A)	Buxton	1 (ST)	Nil
Berkeley Castle	1 (ST)	Nil	Buzzard	1 (BS)*	Nil
Bermuda	1 (ST)	Nil			
Berry Head	1 (ST)	1 (ST)			
Berwick	1 (P)	4 (P), 1 (ST)			
Beverley	1 (ST)	Nil			
Bherunda	1 (ST)	Nil			
Bicester	1 (ST)	Nil			
Bideford	1 (A)	1 (A)			
Bigbury Bay	1 (ST)	Nil			
Birmingham	1 (P)	4 (P)			
Biter	1 (ST)	Nil			
Bittern	1 (A)	2 (A)			
Blackcap	1 (ST)	Nil			
Blackmore	1 (ST)	Nil			
Blackpool	1 (A)	2 (A)			
Black Prince	1 (ST)	Nil			
Black Rover	1 (P)	1 (P)			
Black Swan	1 (A)	2 (A)			
Blackwood	1 (ST)	1 (ST)			
Blue Rover	1 (P)	1 (P)			
Blake	1 (ST)	1 (ST)			
Blanche	1 (D)	2 (D)			
Blankney	1 (ST)	Nil			
Blean	1 (ST)	Nil			
Bleasdale	1 (ST)	Nil			
Blencathra	1 (ST)	Nil			
Blenheim	1 (A)	4 (A)			
Bluebell	1 (A)	2 (A)			
Blyth	1 (A)	Nil			
Boadicea	1 (D)	2 (D)			
Boom Defence	1 (ST)	Nil			
Bonaventure	1 (P)	4 (P)			
Bootle	1 (ST)	Nil			
Boreas	1 (D)	2 (D)			
Boscawen	1 (ST)	Nil			

*The reason for the carving of this badge in the size laid down solely for the use of Capital Ships is not known.

Patterns carved at H.M. Dockyard, Devonport 1982 to date

Name	Screen Badge	Boat Badge
Battleaxe		1 (5″ Dia.)
Bayleaf	1 (ST)	1 (ST)
Beaver	1 (ST)	2 (ST)
Berkeley		1 (ST)
Benbow	1 (ST)	Nil
Biter	1 (12″)	Nil
Black Rover	1 (ST)	1 (ST
Blackwater	1 (ST)	1 (ST)
Blazer	1 (ST)	1 (ST)
Blue Ranger	1 (ST)	1 (ST)
Boscawen	NIL	1 (ST)
Brambleleaf	1 (ST)	1 (ST)
Brave	Nil	2 (ST) and 1 (5″ Dia.)
Brilliant	1 (ST)	1 (ST)

The following existing patterns were modified into Standard Circular Screen Badges:–
Brazen (plus two ST boat-badges) and Berkeley.

In addition to the above, the following miniature badges, (3³⁄₄″ Dia.), were carved for on-board presentations: Battleaxe, Berkeley, Berwick, Bicester, Biter, Blackwater, Blazer, Brazen, Broadsword and Brocklesby.

Abbreviations:– ST – Standard Circular
          A – Auxiliary (Diamond shape)
          P – Pentagonal
          D – Shield Shape
          BS – Battleship (Circular)

BACCHANTE

1

BADSWORTH

2

BAMBOROUGH CASTLE

3

BANGOR

4

BARFLEUR

Submitted

Arthur Cochrane
Clarenceux King of Arms
A.A.H.+

9 August 1944

Passed as
SEALED PATTERN

E.B.C. Dicken
Assistant Controller
for the Board

Admiralty 11 August 1944

5

BARHAM

A.A.H. 098

1

Submitted

Charles H. Hawkes
A.A.H.

25th October 1919

Passed as
SEALED PATTERN

for the Board

Admiralty 19

"Tout Bien ou Rien"

6

BARROSA

Submitted

Arthur Cochrane
Clarenceux King of Arms
A.A.H.

19 February 1946

Passed as
SEALED PATTERN

E.B.C. Dicken
Assistant Controller
for the Board

Admiralty 21st February 1946

7

BASILISK

12

Submitted

A.A.H.

3 June 1929

Passed as
SEALED PATTERN

for CONTROLLER
- 4 JUL
for the Board

Admiralty 4.7.1929

8

A.A.H. 533
24

BASSET

Submitted
A.A.H.
3 December 1934

Passed as
SEALED PATTERN
for the Board
Admiralty 5th March 1935.

"Good Hunting"

9

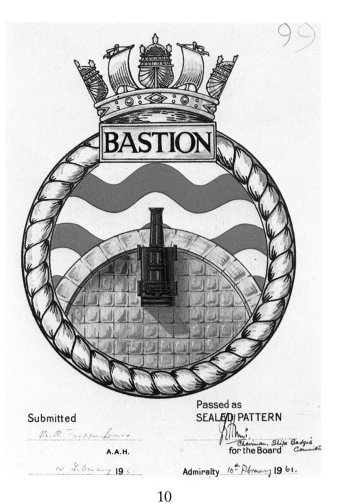

99

BASTION

Submitted
A.A.H.
10 February 1961

Passed as
SEALED PATTERN
Chairman, Ships Badges Committee
for the Board
Admiralty 10th February 1961.

10

75

BATTLE AXE

Submitted
Arthur Cochrane
Clarenceux King of Arms
A.A.H.
25 June 1945

Passed as
SEALED PATTERN
Assistant Controller
for the Board
Admiralty 27th June 1945

11

67

BATTLER

Submitted
Arthur Cochrane
Clarenceux King of Arms
A.A.H.
19

Passed as
SEALED PATTERN
for Deputy Controller
for the Board
Admiralty 12 June 1943

12

BEACHY HEAD

Submitted

Arthur Cochrane
Clarenceux

A.A.H.

2 December 1946

Passed as
SEALED PATTERN

A Madden

for the Board

Admiralty 12 Dec¹ 1946.

13

19

BEAGLE

Submitted

Charles ffoulkes

A.A.H.

3 December 1929

Passed as
SEALED PATTERN

for the Board

Admiralty 6 1 1930

"To a Finish"

14

10/12/38

30

BEATTY

Submitted

A.A.H.

19

Passed as
SEALED PATTERN

for the Board

Admiralty 23.6 1938

15

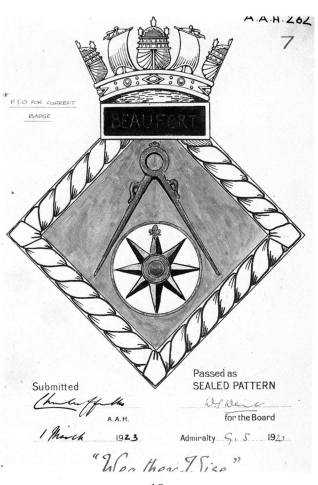

A.A.H. 262

7

P.T.O FOR CORRECT
BADGE

BEAUFORT

Submitted

Charles ffoulkes

A.A.H.

1 March 1923

Passed as
SEALED PATTERN

for the Board

Admiralty 5. 5 1923

"Weather I Rise"

16

+ CORRECT BADGE

51

BEAUFORT

Submitted

A.A.H.

19

Passed as
SEALED PATTERN

for the Board

Admiralty 2 December 1941.

17

BEAULY FIRTH

Submitted

A.A.H.

2 December 1946

Passed as
SEALED PATTERN

for the Board

Admiralty 12 Dec. 1946

18

BEAUMARIS

Submitted

A.A.H.

14 November 19 41

Passed as
SEALED PATTERN

for the Board

Admiralty 18 November 1941

19

109

BEAVER

Submitted

Walter J. Vereo

N.D.A.H.

21 June 1978

Passed as
SEALED PATTERN

for the Board

MOD(N) 21 June 1978

20

BEDALE

21

BEDOUIN

22

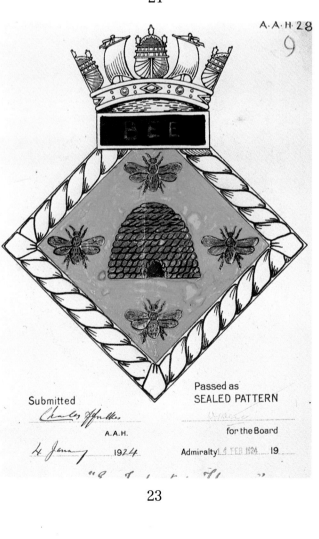

BEE

23

BEGUM

24

25

26

27

28

BELVOIR

Submitted

Arthur Cochrane
Clarenceux King of Arms
A.A.H.

2 June 1942

Passed as
SEALED PATTERN

for Deputy Compt
for the Board

Admiralty 4 June 1942

29

BENBOW

Submitted

Charles ffoulkes
A.A.H.

25 January 1920

Passed as
SEALED PATTERN

Chatfield
for the Board

Admiralty 3 May 1920

30

BEN LOMOND

Submitted

Arthur Cochrane
Clarenceux
A.A.H.

29 June 1949

Passed as
SEALED PATTERN

Fairhead
for the Board

Admiralty June 30th 1949

31

BERKELEY

Submitted

A.A.H.

19

Passed as
SEALED PATTERN

Assistant Controller
for the Board

Admiralty 26th February 1940

32

BERKELEY CASTLE

Submitted

M. R. Trappes-Lomax

A.A.H.

3 April 1954

Passed as
SEALED PATTERN

REAR-ADMIRAL,
CHAIRMAN, SHIPS' BADGES COMMITTEE,
for the Board

Admiralty 15TH APRIL, 1954.

33

BERMUDA

Submitted

Arthur Cochrane
Clarenceux King of Arms

A.A.H.

5 June 1942

Passed as
SEALED PATTERN

for Deputy Garter

for the Board

Admiralty 8 June 1942

34

BERRY HEAD

Submitted

Arthur Cochrane
Clarenceux

A.A.H.

October 15th 1946

Passed as
SEALED PATTERN

for the Board

Admiralty 29 oct. 1946.

35

A.A.H. 290

10

BERRY

Submitted

Charles ffoulkes

A.A.H.

26 July 1924

Passed as
SEALED PATTERN

for the Board

Admiralty 19

"Victoriæ Gloria Merces"

36

BEVERLEY

Submitted

Arthur Cochrane
Clarenceux King of Arms
A.A.H.

24 September 19 41

Passed as
SEALED PATTERN

for Deputy Controller
for the Board

Admiralty 1st October 19 41

37

BHERUNDA

Submitted

Arthur Cochrane
Clarenceux King of Arms
A.A.H.

8 June 19 45

Passed as
SEALED PATTERN

E.B.C. Dicken
assistant Controller
for the Board

Admiralty 11th June 1945

38

BICESTER

Submitted

A.A.H.

19 41

Passed as
SEALED PATTERN

for Deputy Controller
for the Board

Admiralty 12 December 19 41

39

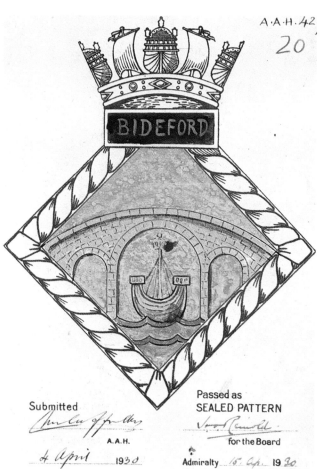

A.A.H. 42
20

BIDEFORD

Submitted

A.A.H.

4 April 1930

Passed as
SEALED PATTERN

for the Board

Admiralty 15 Apr. 19 30

40

41

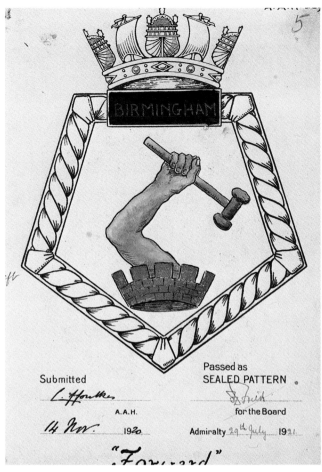

42

43

44

BLACKCAP

45

BLACKMORE

46

BLACKPOOL

47

BLACK PRINCE

48

BLACK SWAN

Submitted

A.A.H.

19

Passed as
SEALED PATTERN

for the Board

Admiralty 13·5 1955

49

BLACKWATER

Submitted

Walter J Verco
N.D.A.H.

3rd July 1984

Passed as
SEALED PATTERN

for the Board

MOD(N) 3rd July 1984.

50

BLACKWOOD

Submitted

M. R. Trappes-Lomax
A.A.H.

10 March 1955

Passed as
SEALED PATTERN

REAR-ADMIRAL
CHAIRMAN, SHIPS' BADGES COMMITTEE
for the Board

Admiralty 28th April, 19 55.

51

BLAKE

Submitted

Arthur Cochrane
Clarenceux
A.A.H.

May 14th 1946.

Passed as
SEALED PATTERN

E.R. Dicken
Assistant Controller
for the Board

Admiralty 16 May 1946

52

BLANCH

Submitted

Charles A. Mulles

A.A.H.

30 July 1929

Passed as
SEALED PATTERN

J. C. Hanley

for the Board

Admiralty 11. 9. 1929

"Dum Spiro Spero"

BLANKNEY

Submitted

Arthur Cochrane
Clarenceux King of Arms

A.A.H.

19

Passed as
SEALED PATTERN

Lionel Dick, for Deputy Controller

for the Board

Admiralty 25 March 1942.

53

54

BLAZER

Submitted

Walter J. Verco

N.D.A.H.

10 June 1985

Passed as
SEALED PATTERN

Buchanan

for the Board

MOD(N) 2 July 1985

BLEAN

Submitted

Arthur Cochrane
Clarenceux King of Arms

A.A.H.

Passed as
SEALED PATTERN

Lionel Dick, for Deputy Controller

for the Board

Admiralty 28 April 1942.

55

56

BLEASDALE

Submitted

Arthur Cochrane
Clarenceux King of Arms
A.A.H.

15 January 1942

Passed as
SEALED PATTERN

for Deputy Controller
for the Board

Admiralty 21 January 1942.

57

BLENCATHRA

Submitted

Arthur Cochrane
Clarenceux King of Arms
A.A.H.

31 March 1942

Passed as
SEALED PATTERN

for Deputy Controller
for the Board

Admiralty 3 April 1942.

58

BLENHEIM

Submitted

C. ffoulkes
A.A.H.

14 Nov. 1920

Passed as
SEALED PATTERN

for the Board

Admiralty 29th July 1921.

59

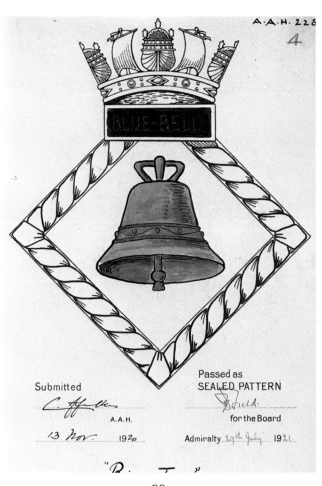

BLUE-BELL

Submitted

C. ffoulkes
A.A.H.

13 Nov. 1920

Passed as
SEALED PATTERN

for the Board

Admiralty 29th July 1921.

60

BLYTH

Submitted
Arthur Cochrane
Clarenceux King of Arms
A.A.H.

19

Passed as
SEALED PATTERN
for the Board

Admiralty 21 *August* 1940

61

BOADICEA

E L Birchall.
DESIGN DIVISION.
DEVONPORT ROYAL DOCKYARD.
30-11-1987.

62

BONAVENTURE

Submitted
Arthur Cochrane
Clarenceux
A.A.H.

19

Passed as
SEALED PATTERN
for the Board

Admiralty 11th *June* 1940

63

BOOTLE

Submitted
Arthur Cochrane
Clarenceux King of Arms
A.A.H.

31 *March* 19 42

Passed as
SEALED PATTERN
for the Board

Admiralty 3 *April* 1942

64

AA H 400   14

BOREAS

Submitted

Charles Joffmiller
A.A.H.

5 June   1929

Passed as
SEALED PATTERN

J. W. Henley
for the Board

Admiralty 4. 7. 1929

"_Vento Favente_"

65

76

BOSCAWEN

Submitted

Arthur Cochrane
Clarenceux
A.A.H.

January 4th 1946.

Passed as
SEALED PATTERN

P. W. C. Dickens
Assistant Controller
for the Board

Admiralty January 8th 1946

66

BOSTON

Submitted

Arthur Cochrane
Clarenceux King of Arms
A.A.H.

15 June   1942

Passed as
SEALED PATTERN

Herbrand for Deputy Controller
for the Board

Admiralty 7 July 1942

67

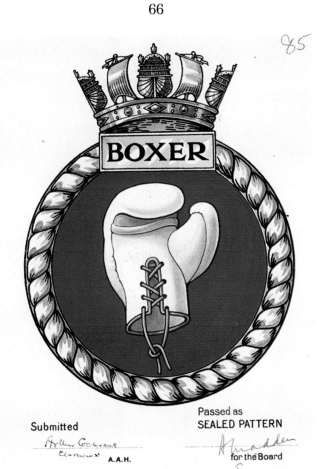

85

BOXER

Submitted

Arthur Cochrane
Clarenceux
A.A.H.

June 30th 1947

Passed as
SEALED PATTERN

Madden
for the Board

Admiralty 3 July 1947

68

BOYNE

Submitted

A.A.H.

21 February 1934

Passed as
SEALED PATTERN
for the Board

Admiralty 23 April 1934.

"Je Maintiendrai"

69

BRADFORD

Submitted

A.A.H.

14 November 1941

Passed as
SEALED PATTERN
for the Board

Admiralty 18 November 1941.

70

BRAMBLE

Submitted

A.A.H.

19

Passed as
SEALED PATTERN
for the Board

Admiralty 13.5.19

71

BRAMHAM

Submitted

A.A.H.

1 December 1941

Passed as
SEALED PATTERN
for the Board

Admiralty 12 December 1941.

72

Submitted

Arthur Cochrane
Clarenceux King of Arms
A.A.H.

14 May 1943

Passed as
SEALED PATTERN

for the Board

Admiralty 21 May 1943

73

Submitted

A.A.H.

7 June 1929

Passed as
SEALED PATTERN

for the Board

Admiralty 4.7.1929

"Audax omnia Perpeti"

74

Submitted

Arthur Cochrane
Clarenceux King of Arms
A.A.H.

6 May 1943

Passed as
SEALED PATTERN

for the Board

Admiralty 8 May 1943

75

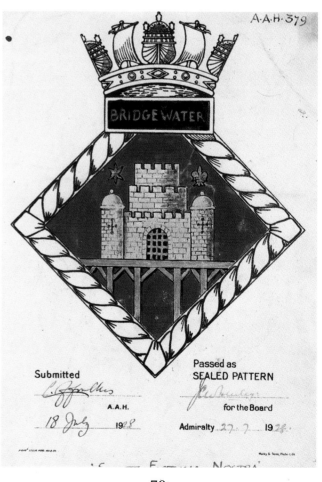

A.A.H. 379

Submitted

A.A.H.

18 July 1928

Passed as
SEALED PATTERN

for the Board

Admiralty 27.7.1928

76

BRIDLINGTON

77

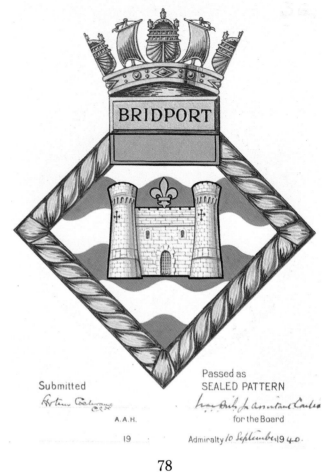

BRIDPORT

78

BRIGHTON

79

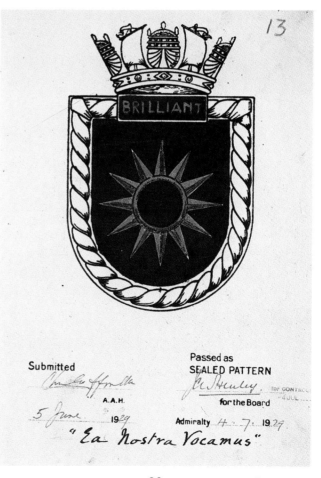

BRILLIANT

13

80

BRISSENDEN

Submitted

Arthur Cochrane
Clarenceux King of Arms
A.A.H. 71

4 October 1942

Passed as
SEALED PATTERN

for the Board

Admiralty 17 October 1942

81

BRITOMART

Submitted

A.A.H.

19

Passed as
SEALED PATTERN

for the Board

Admiralty 13·5 1938

83

BRISTOL

Submitted

A.A.H.

10th February 1909

Passed as
SEALED PATTERN

for the Board

Admiralty 14 February 1969

82

BRIXHAM

Submitted

Arthur Cochrane
Clarenceux King of Arms
A.A.H. 73

3 July 1942

Passed as
SEALED PATTERN

for the Board

Admiralty 7 July 1942

84

BROADSWORD

85

BROCKLESBY

86

BROKE

"Sævum Tridentem Servamus"

87

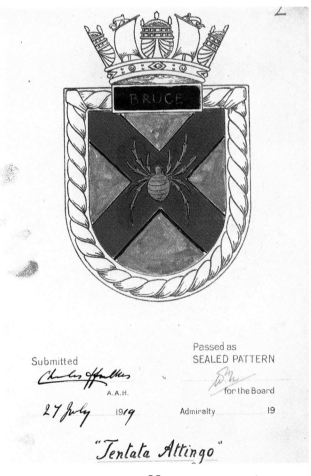

BRUCE

"Tentata Attingo"

88

BRYONY

Submitted

A.A.H.

12 Aug. 1933

Passed as
SEALED PATTERN

for the Board

Admiralty 21st Aug 1933

"FLOREO DUM VIGILO"

89

BUCHAN NESS

Submitted

Arthur Cochrane
Clarenceux King of Arms
A.A.H.

11 March 1946

Passed as
SEALED PATTERN

for the Board

Admiralty 13th March 1946

90

BUDE

Submitted

Arthur Cochrane
Clarenceux King of Arms
A.A.H.

26 January 1942

Passed as
SEALED PATTERN

for Deputy Comb

for the Board

Admiralty 31 January 1942

91

BULAWAYO

Submitted

Arthur Cochrane
Clarenceux
A.A.H.

November 21st 1947

Passed as
SEALED PATTERN

for the Board

Admiralty 24th November 1947

92

BULLDOG

Submitted

A.A.H.

18 August 1929

Passed as
SEALED PATTERN

for the Board

Admiralty   19

"Hold Fast"

93

BULWARK

Submitted

Arthur Cochrane
Clarenceux
A.A.H.

March 19th 1947

Passed as
SEALED PATTERN

for the Board

Admiralty 2 April 1947

94

BURGHEAD BAY

Submitted

Arthur Cochrane
A.A.H.

19th February 1953

Passed as
SEALED PATTERN

Rear Admiral: Chairman, Ships' Badges
for the Board   Committee.

Admiralty 23 February 1953

95

BURNHAM

Submitted

Arthur Cochrane
Clarenceux King of Arms
A.A.H.

5 November   19 41

Passed as
SEALED PATTERN

for Deputy Control
for the Board

Admiralty 11 November 19 41

96

BURWELL

Submitted

~~Arthur Cochrane~~
~~Clarenceaux King of Arms~~
A.A.H.

2ⁿᵈ ~~September~~ 19 4 ?

Passed as
SEALED PATTERN

~~signature~~ for Deputy Controller
for the Board

Admiralty 1ˢᵗ ~~October~~ 1941

97

BUXTON

Submitted

~~Arthur Cochrane~~
~~Clarenceaux King of Arms~~
A.A.H.

13 ~~October~~ 19 41

Passed as
SEALED PATTERN

~~signature~~ for Deputy Controller
for the Board

Admiralty 15 ~~October~~ 1941

98

33.

BUZZARD

Submitted

~~Arthur Cochrane~~
~~Clarenceaux~~
A.A.H.

11ᵗʰ ~~June~~ 1940.

Passed as
SEALED PATTERN

~~signature~~ for the Board

Admiralty 19

99